Dear American Reader,

Hopefully this shouldn't come as too much of a surprise by now, but there's one thing you need to know before you read any further: I'm English. Or, more precisely, I'm an English*man*. There's no need to be alarmed. I'm just like you[1]. Nonetheless, my publisher over here thought it would be a good idea to introduce myself to the American reader just in case you guys don't, you know, 'get' me.

So here's what you should 'get' about me, and English guys in general, before flipping the page to Chapter 1. In spite of whatever English Casanovas you might have seen at the movies (the Bonds, Firths, and Grants etc.), English guys (of which I am a case in point) can be real idiots when it comes to girls. Not jerks, just plain stupid. We may, as you might put it, have 'cute accents,' but that's about as far as it goes when it comes to anything verging on a natural ability to attract members of the fairer sex. We're just as useless at making a move, committing to a relationship, or meeting the parents as just about any other guy you've ever come across.

What you're about to read may not therefore sit very well with any image you may already have of the 'typical' English guy. I mumble, stumble and fumble my way through my love life, with sharp economic analysis only occasionally producing moments of clarity. Nonetheless, I really hope that you enjoy it, and you learn something about love or economics (hopefully both). Writing it, I certainly did.

Yours ever,

William

---

1   OK, not really, but at least we speak the same language (sort of).

The Romantic ECONOMIST

A STORY *of Love* and MARKET FORCES

WILLIAM NICOLSON

MARBLE ARCH
PRESS

MARBLE ARCH
PRESS

Marble Arch Press
1230 Avenue of the Americas
New York, NY 10020

First Marble Arch Press trade paperback edition January 2014

Marble Arch Press is a publishing collaboration between Short Books, UK, and Atria Books, US.

Marble Arch Press and colophon are trademarks of Short Books.

For information about special discounts for bulk purchases, please contact Simon & Schuster Special Sales at 1-866-506-1949 or business@simonandschuster.com.

Illustrations © Andrew Smith 2013
Cover design: Lucy Stephens
Author photo: Ben French

Manufactured in the United States of America

10 9 8 7 6 5 4 3 2 1

ISBN 978-1-4767-3041-7
ISBN 978-1-4767-3042-4 (ebook)

For my parents

Contents

Table of Figures

Chapter 1

Introduction

'I know that this sounds like a cliché, but really, it's not you …'

I stopped listening at this point. I knew what was coming. In my mind I had already dumped myself several times before Lizzie finally got round to doing it. I stared down into my coffee, which had been slowly forming a crust of dried froth, and let the rest come.

'You've been absolutely wonderful. I just don't think I am ready for a serious relationship at the moment.'

She was clever, fun, talented and unbearably beautiful. My mother had already said she wanted me to marry her, but I had lost her in a personal best time of six weeks.

I returned home in a downtrodden, yet contemplative mood. I didn't get it. I couldn't see where I had gone wrong. I had been nothing, or so I thought, but my nicest, funniest and most caring self with her. What seemed to have gone down a treat in the early days quite simply stopped working, practically overnight, around the third week. Suddenly calls went unreturned, kisses were quickly retracted, and eye contact was avoided. If I had wanted the signs to be any clearer they would have had to be written in letters ten feet high. The end was inevitable.

'Perhaps you were *too* nice,' my friend, Flora, playing the shoulder to cry on, suggested to me a couple of days later.

'Don't be ridiculous.'

'You've got to play the game – play hard to get.'

The words 'hard to get' rang in my ears – they reminded me of something. Then it clicked. 'You mean, like, *restrict my supply?*'

She rolled her eyes, a reaction that I was used to getting whenever I translated something, quite unnecessarily, into economic language.

'I guess you could put it like that. But the important thing is that if you give them too much early on they will take you for granted and won't find you attractive.'

I finally understood. 'So, you are saying that I should restrict my supply to *increase my value?*'

'Oh William, please grow up.'

A few days passed. The initial shock began to wear off. Perhaps we weren't right for each other anyway. I was probably more in love with the *idea* of being in love with her than actually in love. Anyhow, I shouldn't really have expected it to end in any other way. I had been at university for a year, and I still hadn't managed to get myself a girl-friend (not one that lasted more than six weeks anyway). I had gone on plenty of dates – some more successful than others – but nothing of any substance had materialised. Whenever I did find a girl I liked, I let my emotions build up too much steam, and she would soon be running for the hills. And yet, in the economics seminar room, I had always prided myself on my ability to think rationally, and get myself out of even the most complex of problems, however many variables or lines of working were involved. Things had to change.

I got thinking about the post-dumping conversation I'd had with Flora. The idea that I had over-supplied myself seemed to have a lot of truth in it: people don't want to go out with someone who just about anyone could get with. You've got to limit your supply, or play hard to get, so that when they do eventually get you it makes them feel special. That simple lesson got me thinking about what else I might be able to learn from applying the economics that I was studying during the day to what I was doing so badly in my spare time: trying to find a girlfriend.

The clear-cut rational world of economics, I thought, must surely be the perfect coolant for my overheated emotions. No longer was I to be the hapless romantic, desperately in search of love, wandering aimlessly from one girl to the next, lost in the mysterious world of women. I was to become an investor in the market for relationships, and use the rational, incisive tools of economics to try to get me a whopping return. Whether this would put me on the path towards enlightenment and eternal happiness, or the fast track to a life plagued by loneliness and dejection – I couldn't say. But one thing was for sure: I would become the *Romantic Economist*.

Chapter 2

About this Book:

Assumptions and Qualifications

I first realised that I needed to introduce the book in this way after I decided to share a few of my ideas with a group of girls at a flat party. I was telling them about supply and demand, or playing hard to get, and it was going pretty well.

'You just need to restrict your supply to increase your price,' I told them, as they gazed at me as if I was some kind of dating sage.

'Amazing, that's *so* true. Tell us more, Will.'

I told them a bit about signalling preferences, bargaining power and inelastic demand. They liked it. Perhaps my idea for a book wasn't so bad after all. Then I went for gold: the efficient market hypothesis.

'Basically, if we assume the market for relationships is perfectly informed, then if you're single, it follows that you're probably single for a reason.'

The looks of awe and admiration I had been basking in for the last fifteen minutes vanished, to be replaced by mingled looks of fury and pity. Evidently all these girls were single, and I had just effectively told them this was because there was something fundamentally wrong with them. I quickly backtracked.

'You do understand that this is just a theory, a theory based on some pretty grandiose assumptions? Of course the market is not perfectly informed. The fact that you three lovely girls are all single is testament to that!'

They had already stopped listening, and were looking for someone, anyone, else to talk to. A friend of mine had been eavesdropping on the last bit of the conversation.

'That's probably the most spectacular crash and burn I've seen you do yet, Will. I'm guessing that's the first time you've tried out that little routine.'

Yes it was a crash and burn, but I did salvage something pretty valuable from the wreckage: I learnt that if you happen not to think like an economist, you will find just about everything an economist says completely wrong, or downright offensive. These girls had taken my conclusion – single girls are single for a reason – to heart (to put it mildly), and ignored the rest of the argument.

As you will discover when you read on, economists like to simplify things (often to absurd degrees), at least to begin with, so that they can uncover hidden truths about the way people behave. Assuming that individuals are rational and self-interested and always perfectly informed is merely a useful first approximation of human nature, which we can then use as a starting point for economic models. If economists started off with people acting the way they did in real life, a combination of rational and irrational, self-interested and altruistic, then our models would be just as complicated as the thing they were trying to explain. We would spend our time drawing life-sized maps of the world, which wouldn't be of any use to anyone.

Over-simplified economic theories which are completely blind to the real world are just as bad. Economists often draw maps that are neat, elegant and easy to read, but they miss out all the smaller roads and subtle contours which are often essential to us reaching our destination. The theory is therefore only half of the battle. The theory provides a benchmark. What would happen *if* we all acted rationally? What would happen *if* we were all perfectly informed? The next step is for us to compare our theory to real life to see whether it is correct, and then to try and explain any inevitable differences.

Some economists fail to take the second step, insisting that it's not their theory that's wrong and needs adjusting, but the world that is misguided. Of course, such an approach can be useful, up to a point. Economists aren't just there to explain why everything is so inefficient, but to suggest ways of improving our lives. John Maynard Keynes liked to compare economists to a dentists, with the difference that the economist uses models and data, rather than drills and fillings, to cure society of its various aches and pains. As social scientists, however, they are also there to explain *why* there is the difference between the theory and reality; what other factors are at play that make us stray from the perfectly rational outcome?

In other words, economists try and explain why markets fail. This is, in a way, what this book is about. But I am not so much asking why markets fail as why my love life has, at times, been such a catastrophe, and seeing if I can use economics to try and put that right. It's a memoir with an economic twist, if you will.

Before getting to the interesting stuff, I am going to lay out my key assumption for the book, and explain a little more about the person that this book is about. *The Romantic Economist* is a bit of an oxymoron. Love and rationality don't mix that well, most of the time. Usually it's the philosophers, psychologists and biologists who tell us about how we fall in love and attract the opposite sex. But I want to offer an alternative account, loosely based on my own experience, in which I assume that we are all self-interested rational individuals, who are simultaneously consumers and suppliers in the market for relationships. We consume the opposite sex, and we are also consumed by them. We all have a market value, and want to get good value, or 'bang for our buck', from what we consume, just like in any other market for goods or services.

Please don't get your hopes up, gents, this is not a book about how to get a girl into a bed. You already have *The Game* for that. Nor is it about money. You won't learn the magic formula that calculates the exact minimum amount of money that you have to spend on your girlfriend to keep her happy. There's a difference between The Romantic Economist and The Unromantic Bastard. It's about a young man trying to make sense of something he doesn't understand, using something that he does. Whether the tools he chooses are always the right ones is another matter.

I'd be the first to admit that applying the language of economics to the world of personal relationships can make us a little uncomfortable. But it's hardly a new concept. The idea that people have a market value, rather than intrinsic, or absolute value, has been around for centuries. Thomas Hobbes, the 17th-century political philosopher says, in *Leviathan*:

> The value or worth of a man is, as of all other things, his price ... therefore is not absolute, but a thing dependent on the need and judgement of another. An able conductor of soldiers is of great price in time of war present or imminent, but in peace not so. A learned and uncorrupt judge is much worth in time of peace, but not so much in war. And as in other things, so in men, not the seller, but the buyer determines the price. For let a man, as most men do, rate themselves at the highest value they can, yet their true value is no more than it is esteemed by others.

What Hobbes is saying here is that we are essentially worthless, and we are only valuable to the extent that others think we are. In short, we are prey to the opinions and demands of the market. One day the market might want blondes, the next brunettes, one day a wit, the next a muscleman, and those blondes and brunettes, those brainboxes and sporting heroes, will see their price vary accordingly.

Evidence of the market for relationships can also be found much closer to home than 17th-century political philosophy. We refer to it in our everyday language. It is common to speak of ourselves as being 'back on the market' when we've recently ended a relationship, or, if we are still in one, going out and flirting with people to be reassured that we 'still have market value'. Similarly, referring to someone as being 'damaged goods' can easily be seen as reference to that person's fall in value, usually after they have been involved in some kind of scandalous affair or traumatic break up.

Online dating is perhaps the most clear-cut example of market principles surfacing in the world of romance. We give a description of ourselves (the goods supplied), and a description of what we want (the goods demanded). Suppliers are then matched up with consumers by the website (the broker). They then go on a first date (the trial period) to see if they want to go out (to trade, exclusively, on a long-term basis).

I appreciate that most of the time this book will only give one side of the story, the man's, but pretty much all the theories in this book can easily be turned on their head to give the female perspective. As we are all simultaneously consumers and suppliers in the market for relationships, and the theories either focus on the supply side (i.e. making yourself more attractive to the opposite sex) or the consumer side (i.e. deciding which person to pursue) each will have a mirror image in which the roles are reversed. I did consider trying to write a balanced account, taking into consideration how men's and women's views might differ, but the problem with that is I am not a woman – a man's perspective is the only one that I can write from honestly and, I hope, insightfully.

I hope – for my sake if no one else's – that having read this section, when you see girls referred to as 'assets' that are 'consumed' or 'invested in' by boys, and time spent with a girlfriend as a 'sunk cost', you won't find your skin crawling quite as much as it otherwise might have done.

Nonetheless, if you still feel the urge to rip up this book at any stage, just try and think like an economist, and bear in mind the assumptions I am making when I arrive at my conclusions. If you do that and still think I am a sexist bastard who exploits and objectifies women, please forgive me.

Chapter 3

Playing Hard to Get:
Supply and Demand

I had made a few fatal blunders with Lizzie. I should, in hindsight, have kept the voicemail from my mum saying that she wanted me to marry Lizzie to myself, rather than playing it to her on speakerphone with a big, cheesy grin on my face. The eight-page letter that I wrote to her after she came to stay at my parents' house, which said pretty much everything but 'I love you', was also probably a bit much, three weeks into a relationship. Flora was right; I had been too nice, and, I admit, verging on obsessive at times. I needed solutions, and why not start at the first page of the textbook: the law of supply and demand.

I'm told that playing hard to get works on some pretty basic principles; don't give away too much early on, don't always be available, wait at least three hours before replying to their texts, etc. 'Treat 'em mean, keep 'em keen', as they say. That makes it sound so simple. But it isn't. It's unbearable self-denial. What's wrong with spending as much time with a girl as you like, and just saying how you feel? Surely just being nice and honest will outweigh any benefit from game playing?

Well, apparently not, and I learnt that the hard way with Lizzie. However nice you are, that niceness will be worthless if you serve it up on plate that can be gobbled down or pushed aside at will.

The fact that we have to play this game to make ourselves more attractive tells us that we are all, apparently, just like any other good; we become more valuable if the demand for us outstrips how much we supply, and decreases if we supply more than is demanded. Therefore playing hard to get, or restricting our supply, increases our price, whereas being too keen, or oversupplying ourselves, decreases it. But here, of course, I don't mean price in the monetary sense. In the market for relationships, someone's price is the amount of effort that we must sacrifice to get with that person. That means that if I am identified as a potential boyfriend by a girl I meet in a club, all other things being equal, the harder I am to get with, the more time, thought and emotion she'll have to invest in order to get with me. The more interest I show in her (i.e. the more I supply), the less effort she'll have to put in to snap me up.

But why should being hard to get necessarily be a good thing? Usually when we try to sell something, and don't find any takers after some time, our natural response is to cut the price, and continue to do so until we find a willing buyer. Playing hard to get, however, results in an increase in price, not a decrease, and yet it is considered a fool-proof method to improve our eligibility. Before I tried following Flora's advice, it was clear that I needed to think about what, in economic terms, I was trying to achieve. A good place to start would be to ask what types of good are more appealing the more expensive they are, rather than the other way round.

Most goods fall into one of two categories: essential goods, or luxury goods. We generally prefer essential goods, such as staple foods, drinks, and household items, to be as cheap as possible, provided that quality is not compromised. No one is going to judge us for our choice of washing up liquid, so we're usually pretty happy to put up with whatever's on offer at the supermarket – the cheaper the better. This is not the case, however, for luxury items, such as jewellery and fast cars, where their relative value not only derives from their quality, but also from their exclusivity. For instance, people buy Rolex watches not necessarily because they tell the time better than, say, a Timex, but because they are beyond the reach of most people. Owning one is a symbol that you have 'made it' (or so Rolex would like people to think). To maintain this status-symbol quality, Rolex makes very few watches, and charges a lot for them. If Rolex increased the number they produced their price would fall, meaning more people would be able to afford them. If too many people could afford a Rolex, however, then the quality that made them attractive in the first place, exclusivity, would be under-mined, and the rich would look elsewhere for another watch to show the world how marvellous they are.

When it comes to marketing yourself as a potential boyfriend (or, in the Lizzie case, a boyfriend that a girl wants to stay with), it looks like playing hard to get is, in part, as for Rolex watches, an effort to maintain your status as a luxury good. We want to brand ourselves as boys that only the very best of girls would be able to get with and to make that girl feel as though they have gained exclusive access to our affections. Giving yourself to a girl in your entirety from the word go may be nice for them to begin with, but soon they will be thinking, 'is he like this with every girl he meets?' or worse, '*does everyone else know* that he's like this with every girl that he meets?' For one's affections to come too easily makes the girl feel that just about anyone else could have, or already has, been in their shoes, and their reputation as someone who has 'made it' will suffer. Rather than making them feel like they're wearing a Rolex, if you're like putty in their hands from day one, they'll feel like they're parading the latest Casio (and not even a fashionable vintage one).

The Thursday night after Lizzie dumped me was the perfect opportunity to put this theory to the test; it was time to play the game. First of all, given my newly single status, I had to deal with some rather predictable taunts during the warm-up drinks:

'Will's on the rebound – clearly out on the pull tonight!', 'Will's single again – look out, girls, he's coming for you!' and 'Ooh that's your third, Will, trying to pluck up some Dutch courage, are we?!'

I guess that's what friends are for. They stop you worrying about life's problems and your insecurities by ripping them out of you and trampling all over them. No need for the time-consuming, softly-softly approach.

We hit the club. Judging by the number of girls at the bar, it looked like there'd be plenty of opportunities to get things back on track. I tried to plan some approaches, but all I could think of were Flora's words, 'You were too nice – play hard to get.' I started psyching myself up; *I am a luxury brand, not an essential good. There simply won't be enough of me to go around – the girls will be queuing up by the end of the night.* With these thoughts racing through my mind, I spotted a rather nice looking girl standing by herself at the bar, and went for it.

'Hi, I'm Will, having a good night?'

She seemed slightly taken aback by such a direct line, but smiled nonetheless.

'Yeah, not too bad – just got a big piece of coursework in so am letting off some steam.'

'Well that makes two of us. Can I get you a drink?'

'Sure – vodka lemonade please. I'm Rebecca by the way.'

We hadn't been talking for long, but seemed to be hitting it off. I already felt relaxed with her, generally like I was being myself. But then I realised that wasn't the plan. I was being too nice. I had to cut this conversation short if I was going to stand any chance of getting with her.

'Rebecca, it was really nice meeting you but I've just seen some friends of mine that I haven't seen for ages. I might see you later for another drink,' I said, already walking off to the next room in my friends' direction.

She glanced down at her drink, which was still three-quarters full. She looked slightly unsettled by the abruptness of my exit; I had timed it perfectly.

'Yeah sure, might see you later then,' I just about caught her saying as I found myself reunited with the boys.

'She seemed all right, Will. Why have you left her by herself at the bar? Don't let us stop you going for her – rebound away.'

'Yeah she's nice. But I just wanted to give her a teaser. I'm playing hard to get.'

Freddie, my flat mate and one of my best friends, spat out his drink.

'Playing hard to get? Will, you do understand that we're in a club. You haven't got time to play hard to get. If you play hard to get someone else will beat you to it.'

'Don't you worry. You'll see. I've got everything under control.'

I didn't even think for a moment that Freddie had a point. I knew what I was doing. I had economics on my side, after all.

There was about half an hour till closing, by which point the club had grown thick with sweat and alcohol, and the floor had become sticky with stray sambuca shots, leaving a scent of sweet aniseed just about anywhere you went. I hadn't seen Rebecca since I left her stranded at the bar, hours earlier. I finally caught a glimpse of her, chatting to another guy by the exit leading out to the smoking area. My plan was to head over and try to catch her eye as I walked past, in the hope of our initial attraction at the beginning of the night pulling her away. It looked like this guy was getting it all wrong anyway – he was being far too keen, leaning over her with one arm up against the wall. I bought a couple of drinks to show that I wasn't by myself, and headed in their direction.

The first passing had no impact whatsoever. It was an air shot. She didn't even look at me. I just walked straight past her, my raised eyebrows not even providing the most short-lived of diversions. I found myself outside with noone to talk to, sipping away at my drinks.

'Looking for someone, Will?'

'Freddie, hey.' I was, in part, relieved to see him, but I also knew I was about to be on the receiving end of some pretty predictable I-told-you-so smugness.

'Who's that other drink for? The girl you've got "under control"?'

'Yes, actually.'

'And why are you holding it?'

'She's talking to that guy over there.'

Freddie looked over at Rebecca. Having that other drink with me seemed to be the last thing on her mind. But they weren't standing within lunging distance yet, so I still had time.

'Oh, I see. Looks like you're taking that hard-to-get thing quite seriously. You're making her guess when you've got a drink for her. Let me know how that one goes. I'm off.'

It was time for the second passing. This time it would be slower. I was sure the first time had been just a bit too subtle – eyebrow-raising clearly wasn't enough in a dark and noisy club. I walked over to the entrance, but a bouncer suddenly provided a rather large, unexpected obstacle.

'No glasses allowed outside, mate.'

'Well that's lucky because I'm just taking them inside now.'

'Don't try and be clever with me. What were you doing with them outside then? You know the rules,' he said, pointing to a NO GLASSES OUTSIDE sign by the door.

'Ok, I'm sorry. I get the point. Is it all right for me to go back inside now?'

'I'm going to have to take those off you, I'm afraid.'

'Really? But I'm taking them inside. I've paid for them.'

'I've already said don't try and be clever with me. Now just give me the drinks or I'm going to have to escort you from the premises.'

'I'm not trying to be clever, I'm just …'

The bouncer turned away and mumbled something into his radio. He was calling for reinforcements.

Two more bouncers appeared.

'What's the problem, Rich?'

'Get this guy out of here.'

Both bouncers, one short and stocky with a neatly trimmed goatee beard, the other larger and bull-headed, moved in to seize their prey.

By now I had a small audience. And who could blame them? Watching a stranger getting chucked out of a club is always pretty entertaining, particularly when you know they haven't actually done anything wrong.

I got bundled out of the club, spilling both drinks all over my shirt in the process. I caught a glimpse of Rebecca, who looked pretty amused at the sight of a helpless boy, his shirt soaked through with vodka cranberry, being dragged out of club by two men.

Things hadn't really gone to plan on my first Romantic Economist night out. Freddie, as much as I hate to admit, was probably right. Playing hard to get in clubs doesn't really work – there's so much competition that any attempt to increase your price might actually make you less attractive. If other guys are offering similar goods in terms of their looks and small talk, but are not playing hard to get, they are clearly offering a better deal. Although Rebecca liked me, at first, she wasn't up for chasing me around a club when she could get the same for less elsewhere.

I went back to Flora to discuss where things had gone wrong.

'Flora, that whole playing-hard-to-get thing didn't really work out for me last night.'

'Will, what exactly were you trying to do?'

'Well I started talking to this girl at the bar, we were getting on pretty well, but then I remembered what you said – I was being *too* nice, so I cut the conversation short, and the next time I saw her she was with some other guy.'

Flora rolled her eyes at me, something I was getting pretty used to in all the girl talks we'd been having recently. What she said next confirmed my suspicions – I had played hard to get at the wrong time and in the wrong place.

'Will, you're an idiot. You can only play hard to get once the girl actually knows and likes you – in a club you're just a stranger.'

'Oh, I get it. You can only restrict your supply once you've established a monopoly.'

'Will, I think you should probably drop the whole economics crap – I don't think it's really helping.'

'No, I think I see it now. In a club there's perfect competition. If you price yourself too highly, then others will undercut you and get the consumer you're after. Girls are happy to substitute one guy they meet at the bar for another if they think they can get more or less the same thing without having to put in as much effort...'

'OK, Will, you're boring me now. Why don't you just give it a go when you find a girl you like, and who likes you, maybe after a date or two, and see what happens. And if you mention restricting your supply, or increasing your price one more time, I genuinely fear that you might never have a girlfriend ever again.'

I took my theorising elsewhere. What I was just beginning to understand was that I had to adapt my tactics to suit the situation, or, more precisely, the market structure. What I mean by market structure is how many players there are in a particular market, and what level of control some of those players have in terms of setting the market price. Generally speaking, if there are lots of companies in a market selling the same thing (*homogenous goods*), then no one company will be able to control the market price (they are *price takers*). In such a market, consumers, assuming that they know how much each company is selling the goods for, will purchase the goods from the company that sells them for the lowest price. Any company that decides to sell at a higher price than the rest will attract no customers and will go out of business, and will effectively be powerless to charge more than the rest of the market. If there is only one company in the market (i.e. a monopoly), however, then, as they have no one else to compete with, the company will have complete control over the market price (they are *price setters*). If a monopolist decides to increase the price they are charging, then consumers will generally have to put up with the increase, as they can't turn to other companies to get the same goods for less.

To see what this means in practice, let's take the example of the non-premium lager market, where there are several beer companies, each offering a practically identical product. When a guy orders a drink at the bar and is presented with a choice of Fosters, Carlsberg or Carling, as he can't really tell the difference in flavour between them, he is going to go for the cheapest one. As a result, each company will make sure that they don't price their beer above that of their competitors. In such a homogenous goods market, consumers are said to have a high *price-elasticity of demand*, meaning that their consumption choices are very sensitive to changes in price.

Rebecca, the girl I met in the club, was clearly such a consumer. There were lots of average-looking guys like me, and she didn't know enough about any one of them to be able to tell them apart. Therefore all she had to go on was price. Just like a drinker ordering a lager at the bar, if she thought that we were more or less all going to be the same she would go for the cheapest one, i.e. the one that she had to sacrifice the least amount of effort to get with. This usually means the one who is putting in the most work to get with her (i.e. the one I thought was being 'too keen'), not the one playing hard to get (i.e. me).

Things are different, however, when there is a difference between the goods on offer. As Flora mentioned, you can only play hard to get once the girl actually knows and likes you. This is because by then you have differentiated yourself from the other boys on the market, and you gain more control over your market price (you change from a price taker to a price setter). As you come to be seen as an individual with unique characteristics, rather than one of many boys trying to get some action in a club, the market structure changes from one of many competitors selling homogeneous goods to one of a handful of competitors, or even one, selling differentiated goods.

We can see how this affects our consumption decisions by going back to the example of the lager market. In addition to the non-premium lagers (your Fosters, Carlsbergs and Carlings), most pubs will have a range of premium continental lagers (your Peronis, Amstels, and Becks). The premium lagers are stronger, have more flavour, and usually come in a trendily shaped glass or 'chalice'.[1] Because of these distinctive qualities, beer drinkers are willing to pay considerably more for a premium lager than their non-premium counterparts. If pubs decide to take advantage of this taste for fine lagers and increase their price by, say, 10 percent, they will probably find their patrons will be willing to part with an extra 40p or so to keep on drinking their favoured tipple. This is clearly different to a scenario where only non-premium lagers are on offer. There, because demand is more elastic, any increase in price makes drinkers switch brand. Here, because drinkers feel that distinctive qualities of premium lager continue to justify its extra cost, demand is said to be less elastic or, if the consumer is particularly tolerant of increases in price, even *inelastic*.

If the pub, however, encouraged by their patrons' apparent loyalty to the premium lagers, then decides to increase their price again by 20 percent, the patrons are more likely to walk out the door in outrage than to suck

---

1   Perhaps the grisliest word in modern marketing.

up the extra cost. They'd probably think that not even the tastiest beer in the world would be worth paying more than £5 a pint for, and they would either switch to drinking cat's piss (sorry Fosters, Carling, and Carlsberg), or change pub altogether. They might not get the same depth of flavour by drinking non-premium lager (or the trendy glass), but at least it's still cold, fizzy, refreshing, and vaguely beer-flavoured. Paying an extra £2 to get a beer with added flavour is simply not worth it. In other words, their demand for premium lager may be less elastic than for non-premium lager, but there will come a point where drinkers feel that the extra cost is no longer justified, and they will get better 'bang for their buck' by drinking worse beer.

I felt I was finally getting to the bottom of this whole playing hard to get thing. What I had already learnt was that this tactic was only suited to at least the second or third date phase, because only then was demand sufficiently inelastic for a girl to tolerate, or even be attracted to, a rise in price. But, with the help of my beer-drinking analogy, it was now clear that there must be some limit to how hard to get one could be and still have girls yearning after you. If you restrict your supply too much then there will come a point where the girl says 'enough is enough'. However great or unique a guy you are, if you're impossible to pin down, then girls will start looking elsewhere for similar goods at a lower price, even if getting a better deal means they have to give up some of your harder to come by qualities. Rather like an Amstel or Peroni drinker, while girls may be happy to sacrifice more to get the premium product, there is a limit to what they will be willing to pay.

I recalled that Flora had once had a boyfriend who had fallen off the end of the hard-to-get scale in this way. She had met a guy, a good-looking Parisian student called François, while inter-railing around Europe. She had managed to keep up a long distance relationship for eight months, but had eventually called it a day after she came to realise that he simply wasn't worth the effort, however harsh that may sound. She said that the time they spent apart – while at first it had made her long for him even more – in the end created a mental block between them. Over time, their thoughts drifted elsewhere, and their daily Skype chat soon turned into a weekly one, and then into a bi-weekly one, before they finally admitted to themselves that the relationship was no longer sustainable.

In this scenario, Flora had initially seen her demand for François rise the longer they spent apart, but then,

FIGURE 1: Girl's demand for boy over time spent apart

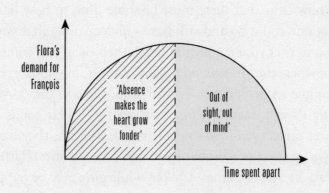

eventually, come crashing down when they had spent so long apart that the relationship became too expensive (in effort terms, rather than the cost of Eurostar tickets, although those were also a bit of a killer) to sustain. Over the course of eight months, their feelings had gone from 'absence makes the heart grow fonder' to 'out of sight, out of mind.' Figure 1 shows how these emotions evolved.

Here the first half of the story is one of scarce resources; the less available François became, the more Flora was willing to sacrifice to stay with him. The second half, however, is one of *cross-price elasticity of demand*; there came a point where, however great François was as a boyfriend, he was simply too unobtainable, and Flora was better off looking elsewhere for someone else who, while perhaps not as well-dressed, intelligent and good-looking, required much less effort to be with, and therefore presented a more attractive overall package. Alternatively, of course, it might just have been that François's sense of humour wasn't really suited to Skype conversations. His quick-witted quips that had gone down so well in the flesh in the cafés and bars of Paris were now rendered completely ineffective by a fatal half-second delay, which meant that Flora would only hear his humorous remark on what she had just told him when she was already half way through her next sentence. The long, bewildered pauses and confused cross-over of voices that inevitably ensued must have become too awkward for Flora to bear. Or perhaps it was simply that his usually chiselled features just didn't look that good in pixelated form.

Whatever the reason for the demise of Flora and François's relationship, one thing was already clear to me;

I could theorise all I liked about why a boy and a girl's feelings for one another could swell and contract over time, but this was completely useless if I didn't have a girl to try and apply my new way of thinking to. My first effort had clearly floundered – emphatically. If only I knew then what I know now. But I was still learning, and, it seemed, things could only get better.

Chapter 4

Too Good to be True:
The Efficient Market Hypothesis

I looked everywhere I could for a suitable candidate. I scanned the library, student bars, and lecture theatres, but whenever someone caught my eye and I made enquiries as to their availability they were, without exception, taken. I learnt that some had even been in relationships since freshers' week and remained so ever since. Clearly there wasn't going to be a quick fix to the problem.

I thought my luck had changed one evening at our usual pre-Thursday night gathering at Wetherspoons. She suddenly appeared before me, as if from nowhere, and introduced herself.

'Hi, I'm Emma, I've seen you around but I don't think we've ever met.'

She was absolutely gorgeous. She had long wavy reddish-brown hair, intense green eyes, and a certain bubbliness to her that instantly attracted me.

I had said nothing for a lot longer than I realised.

'Sorry, I'm Will, nice to meet you.'

'Funny how we've been here well over a year and yet we're still meeting new people.'

'I know, I can't believe that I haven't met anyone as, well, anyone like you before now.'

She giggled in the most adorable way, while I tried not to appear as if I was already a little bit in love.

'Can I get you a drink?'

'How kind of you to offer me a drink in Wetherspoons! Yes, let's.'

I liked this girl. She was beautiful, fun, and she was flirting with me. How could this be? I was certain that by now all the good ones were taken. My friends would kill me if they found out I had got with this girl. I could see their faces now, green with envy. 'You've lucked-out there, Will,' they would say, scrunching their fists in their pockets.

We had a couple of drinks. It felt good. We were comfortable, and clearly attracted to each other. There was plenty of hair flicking, shoulder touching, and prolonged eye contact. I was in there.

'Listen, it's been great meeting you Will, but I said I would go to a friend's flat party tonight – it's her birthday. Can I get your number? Would love to go for a drink sometime. Next Tuesday perhaps?'

She had taken the lead: just my type. We exchanged numbers and went our separate ways. But I couldn't stop thinking about her. She had left an indelible mark. I thought about her parting words to me. A drink on a Tuesday night – not a typical night to go out. That suggested that she wanted to spend time alone with me; she didn't plan on merging the date with a night-out with her friends afterwards. This was the real thing. 'I've found her,' I thought. Or perhaps she had found me. Either way,

I was excited about our next meeting, and I think she was too. Had I found the girl that I had been yearning for all this time? Or was she too good to be true?

We exchanged a couple of flirty texts in the build up to the date. I fought hard to hold back any soppiness – it was far too early to give much away, so I relied on the emotion-neutral territory of cliché:

Me: Hey Emma, so are we still on for that drink on Tuesday? I am game if you are. X

Emma: Sure am! Where do you want to go? Xx

Me: Great. I've got a few places in mind – do you want to start at The Royal Oak and see where the night takes us? X

Emma: I like the sound of that. Meet you there at 8? X

Me: Yep. Look forward to it![2] X

It was 8.15 and she still hadn't arrived. I sat in the corner without a drink so as not to draw attention to myself as a potential stood-upee. At 8.30 there was still no sign. Now I could safely call her to see if everything was OK without coming across as neurotic.

'Hi Will! I am *so* sorry I am running a bit late [*a bit late*?]. I've been caught up with friends. I'll be with you in ten minutes. Just getting on a bus now. I am so, so sorry. I

2   That final exclamation mark was probably a bit much, looking back on it.

will buy you a drink to make up for it when I arrive.'

She was going to be late, and hadn't let me know. A bit annoying, but she sounded pretty adorable nonetheless. I perked up, and bought a drink now that the risk of being stood-up had all but passed.

She arrived half an hour later, apologising profusely.

'Oh my God, Will, I am so sorry. Sooo sorry. Tubes were a nightmare.'

I was sure she had said she was getting the bus, but I let it slide. We kissed on both cheeks. I could smell hints of the delicious perfume she wore when we first met, only this time it was infused with alcohol.

'Don't worry about it, Emma. What can I get you to drink?'

'I'd love a double gin and tonic.'

Double? It was only a Tuesday night. She was clearly on a mission, and why the hell not. Exams were a mile off, and these were some of most care-free days we would ever have.

'Good shout. Let's make that two.'

We slurped down our gin and tonics. I tried to start more or less where we had finished off, fumbling around for the connection that I thought we had made on the night we met. But it wasn't there. She wasn't picking up the references to our previous conversation, and she seemed fidgety, chewing the end of her straw like a child. She looked away when she spoke to me, only making eye contact when she had finished what she was saying.

Was this some kind of game that she played with boys? Draw us in with her big green eyes and endearing giggles, and then give us nothing but a brick wall when we came back for more? The pre-date nerves that had eluded me before the drink began to surface. I became self-conscious, unsure of myself, and lost track of the conversation.

But then, suddenly, things took a turn for the better.

'Let's get another drink. Then how do you feel about going out? It's ages since I last went dancing.'

My heart lifted. 'Sounds great, but where did you have in mind? It's a Tuesday – no one goes out on a Tuesday.'

'Don't worry about that. I know a place. Do you want to get a couple of shots in while I just pop to the loo?'

'Sure. Sambuca?'

'I'd rather die. Vodka,' she said as she lifted herself out of her seat.

It was then that I realised how drunk she was. Her heel keeled over to one side as she collided with the bar, before she quickly corrected herself. My hopes that I had found someone special were draining away. In fact, it looked like I had a liability on my hands.

We did our shots and jumped in a cab. She didn't hang around once we got moving. She lunged straight for me. Her tongue was everywhere, wind-milling around my mouth as if she wanted to map each and every contour of my gum line. I didn't really know what to do, so just went along with it. We kissed like teenagers at their first disco, pausing only for breath and a quick wipe of the mouth. It was kind of exciting, albeit in an unhygienic way.

We arrived at the club. The place was heaving with indie kids; the guys were wearing more make-up than the girls, and to describe the cut of some people's jeans as 'skinny' would be a gross understatement.

'Right, wait here, I just need to pop to the girls'.'

I dutifully stood a few feet from the loos. The first ten minutes went by pretty quickly. I was quite happy to tap my feet and nod my head to some old favourites from Oasis, Blur and Arcade Fire. I was a little more concerned after fifteen minutes. Must just be a big queue, I thought. The place was pretty rammed after all.

After half an hour, I was beginning to sober up. Had she done a runner and jumped out of a window? That's what I thought for about five minutes, before I realised we were in a basement. After 45 minutes I finally decided to do what no man can rightfully do in ordinary circumstances; I put my head down and went in to find her.

'What the hell are you are doing in here?' said a girl wearing inside-out jeans.[3]

'I've lost my girlfriend, I think she's passed out in here.'

'Slipped something into her drink, have we?'

'No, I just think she's had one too many.'

'Get the hell out right now or I'm getting the bouncer.'

'Hang on. I don't know what your problem is, but my girlfriend might be choking to death on her own vomit. Just let me have a look for her.'

'Yeah, whatever, pervert,' the girl said under her breath, finally leaving me in peace.

I then endured the rather undignified process of looking under each of the cubicles for a passed-out Emma. After nothing but a few pairs of knickers wrapped around

---

3 A classic alternative look, apparently.

ankles, I found her curled up around a loo in the last cubicle but one. I prodded her from the other side of door. Nothing. I shouted her name, but that only attracted a small crowd of girls, curious as to what a blue-shirted boy was doing on all fours on the filthy, partially flooded floor (I am guessing it was just water, given that this was a girls' loo).

I reached further under the door and used a little trick I had learnt from a paramedic to stir even the most paralytic of clubbers; a finger pressed firmly in the pit behind the ear lobe. It worked. She regained consciousness and got to her feet, then sheepishly opened the cubicle door.

I didn't show her much sympathy.

'Come on, let's get you home,' I said, taking her by the arm.

The bus ride back to hers was miserable. She drifted in and out of consciousness, while I tried to elicit some kind of apology from her. But my rage was only made worse by her lack of response.

'You know I was standing outside for 45 minutes, Emma.'

Her head swayed in circles, her eyes half-open.

'Do you have any idea how worried I was about you?'

I was talking to her like she was a girlfriend who had misbehaved. But she wasn't that at all. She was just a girl who had drifted into my life one evening, momentarily shifting all my hopes and expectations, and then she, or rather the girl I thought I had met, was gone. She had seemed too good to be true at the time, and she turned out to be exactly that.

I got Emma to her front door and held her up as she

fumbled through her handbag for her keys. After a minute of manic rummaging,[4] she decided to tip the whole thing out on the floor, smashing a half-empty small bottle of vodka in the process. She identified her keys among the alcohol-soaked debris, opened the door and quickly pulled it shut behind her, leaving me standing by myself in the hallway.

I tried knocking for a few minutes, shouting for her to let me in. She wasn't in a state even to put herself to bed – I couldn't just leave her. But then, as if my Tuesday night couldn't get any worse, her next-door neighbour, a greying middle-aged woman, appeared in her dressing gown.

'Excuse me. Do you have any idea what time it is? Some of us have to work tomorrow you know.'

I tried to appear as civil as I could in dealing with this perfectly reasonable complaint. But it didn't really come out that way – I lost it.

'Do you have any idea what I've been through tonight? There's a girl in there who might be choking to death on her own vomit.'[5]

Before the lady had any chance to response to my outburst, Emma, right on cue, shouted at me through the door, 'Go home, Will!'

'I think you'd better,' the lady said.

Without apologising, I gladly took her advice and headed down the stairs.

'You're not the first, by the way, if that makes it any better,' she said, just before I got to the door.

---

4   Why on earth don't girls compartmentalise their handbags?
5   I can't quite believe that I had to make this excuse twice in one night.

Hardly.

However ridiculous this may sound, somehow I now felt this end was inevitable. Beautiful, fun, intelligent, *single* girls don't just appear out of nowhere like that. I should have known that the encounter would be doomed from the beginning. I called Freddie the next day to tell him about the first date from hell.

'Freddie, you won't believe what a mess I got into last night. I went for a drink with this girl Emma ...'

'Are we talking about the red-head Emma? Really fit but a complete mental case?'

'Yes, she has red hair but I didn't know about the mental case bit. Not until last night anyway.'

'Let me guess, she got ridiculously drunk and passed out somewhere.'

'Er, yeah, that is what happened. How did you know?'

'Will, she's a complete disaster area. "Ground Zero" a few people call her – she's a total liability with drink. Gets around a bit, too. Oh yeah, and she's a compulsive liar.'

'Ah, well that explains last night then.'

I told Freddie the whole story, from the great expectations on Thursday night to the misery of the night before. He wasn't surprised, or sympathetic for that matter.

'Will, did you honestly think that you could get that lucky? Were you not slightly suspicious of the fact that she was still single? No offence, but you should have seen it coming.'

There's a saying that exactly summed up my situation; you never pick up a £50 note off the street, because the chances are that someone else would have picked it up already. In other words, if you come across something that you cannot quite believe, something that seems too good to be true, then it is. This is because in a world of scarce resources, when something is worth having you are either made to pay dearly for it, or, if it is under-priced, it is snapped up by someone else before you can even reach for your wallet.

Bargains don't just come up to you in the pub and say, 'Hello, nice to meet you.'

The reason that bargains can be so hard to come by is that, in a competitive market, prices generally reflect how much an asset is actually worth, a theory known as the *efficient market hypothesis*. The theory rests, crucially, on the assumption that the market is perfectly informed, so that everyone in that market has the same information about the assets being traded. This means that if something is cheap, the market believes it is not an asset particularly worth having (in comparison to what else is on offer), whereas if something is expensive, then the market believes that it is.

The effect of this is to make it hard to make a big profit on any particular trade. For example, if a commodities trader discovers that there has been a particularly bad orange harvest and expects the price of oranges to increase tomorrow as a result, he will buy oranges today while they are still cheap and try to sell them for a profit tomorrow following their rise in price. As all commodity traders know about the bad harvest, however, any profit that the trader would have made is wiped out, as all the traders buy oranges today making the price, which was expected to rise tomorrow, rise today. Only the traders who get in there early are therefore able to make any meaningful profit, while the traders who are slower off the mark can only break even (more or less).

The perfectly informed market used to be a bit of a myth, existing only in academic textbooks, and, to a large extent, it still is. But in some circumstances, a combination of technology and market regulation has made it as close to a reality as is practically possible.

The stock market is one such example. Each company which has its shares listed on the stock market is obliged by law to reveal certain information about itself that may affect its share price, such as the loss of a major contract, disputes it's involved in with other companies, or plans to take over another company. There are also heavy penalties, including prison, for those who spread false information about a certain company in the hope of distorting its share price (*market abuse*), as well as for those who try and exploit information about a certain company that is only known to a small number of people (*insider trading*).

The idea behind these regulations is to give everyone in the market equal access to reliable and accurate information about the companies whose shares they are trading. This means, in theory, that if a company appears to be majorly undervalued, it isn't; the market will have factored in all information available about that company and its share price will closely reflect how much it is actually worth.

So if you think you've stumbled across a bargain, something that everyone else seems to have missed, the chances are that you'll be in for an unpleasant surprise.[6]

These principles also apply to the market for relationships. Like in all other markets, we rely on information to decide what we want to buy in that market (who we want to go out with) and at what price (how much effort we're willing to put in to get with them). When the market is generally poorly informed about which girls are available, if you do find a girl with relationship potential, you'll be in a position to make her your girlfriend without having to fight off too much competition from other boys. In other words, you can grab a bargain quite easily. The more the rest of the market becomes informed, however, then the amount of effort that boys are willing to put in to get with the more desirable girls increases, and the amount of effort that people are willing to put in to get with the less desirable girls decreases. In other words, the market becomes more efficient; the amount of effort that people are willing to put in to get with others becomes proportionate to how desirable that person would be to have as a girlfriend or boyfriend.

When I first started university, I was in a poorly informed market for relationships. Nobody knew anyone, and so all we really had to go on was looks and small talk. This was, in part, why it was such an exciting time to be single; if you found a girl on a night out, chatted her up, and pulled, there was every chance that she might be the

6   Of course, in reality, even in very well regulated markets with strict disclosure requirements, some people are better informed than others, or are better at interpreting that information, meaning that there are plenty of undervalued (and overvalued) stocks where traders can make, (or lose) an awful lot of money. See Chapter 10 on investment for more about how we can profit from *inefficient* markets.

girl of your dreams. Alternatively, she could be a complete psycho.

I remember there being one particularly nice girl, Laura, who emerged after the first week as being the girl to get with. The boys circled her like predators, albeit in a charming and flirtatious way. It was quite amusing to watch as they fell over each other to buy her a drink, or swoop in as soon as another momentarily left her side. But out of nowhere, one boy emerged victorious after the third week. How did he achieve such a feat? It wasn't necessarily because he was the nicest, best looking of the bunch. Far from it, in fact. It was just, unbeknown to the rest of us, he was the one who had got in there on the first night, and they had both managed to keep it quiet ever since. He had seen a market opening and put in the effort before the rest of the market was even aware of the opportunity. Freddie was pretty pissed off.

'Lucky catch. He doesn't deserve her – she could do so much better.'

Had she waited a little bit longer she would have realised that this was the case, but as this lucky boy had invested early, and she didn't want to suffer the reputational damage of switching between boys so early on in her university career, she was tied up, for now.

Eighteen months on, the market conditions were very different. Over time, as those in my year got to know each other, the market became better informed and more efficient; through repeated interaction, experience and gossip (and the odd bit of Facebook stalking), boys got together with girls who were more suited to them and vice versa. That meant that all the good ones were taken (after the boys put in a proportionate amount of effort to get with them), and all the remaining single girls were single because no one was competing for them, probably for a good reason.

My experience in the girls' loos with Emma, an attractive, suspiciously single girl, suggested that she had been correctly priced by the market. Boys generally aren't willing to pay a high price, or put in a lot of effort, for a girl who has a habit of turning a night out into an A&E ordeal. But what did that say about me? After a year and a half on the lookout, I was still single. Was I fairly priced? Was I worth putting in the effort for? My single status was fast becoming a self-fulfilling prophecy; if you're single, it's probably because you wouldn't make a good boyfriend. I needed to show the market that I had been undervalued, and that I was an asset waiting to be discovered.

Chapter 5

The 'You'll Do' Horizon:

Market Power

I was having a coffee between lectures with Flora talking about my girl problems as usual. But then, out of nowhere, she asked me whether I would marry her. There were, I should add, two conditions: it could only happen when she had reached the age of 30, and if we were both still single.

'My, what a question,' I said, wondering whether this was some kind elaborate chat-up line. Playing along, I replied, 'But what if I am a total failure, what if I am still living with my parents and can't afford our first home? Would you still want to marry me then?'

'I'm sure you'd do.'

'Flora, I'm flattered. It's a deal.'

Whether or not this proposal was supposed to be a joke, it did reflect the way a lot of people, both girls and boys, think when it comes to marriage. As the prospect of a life alone becomes more realistic, we are willing to settle for someone who falls progressively shorter of our idea of perfection. In our early twenties only absolute perfection would do; by the time we are 30 we are all ready to compromise. Being with someone, anyone, is better than being that single man or woman who still has to be invited round to their friends' family homes for Christmas Day aged 45. That was why Flora was asking me this now, aged 21. She didn't want to end up scraping the barrel at her friends' weddings for a man from a diminishing pool of eligible bachelors.

I was too young to know this from first-hand experience, but I am told that for various reasons, some biological, some social, this pressure to get married by a certain age is generally greater on girls than on boys. The straightforwardly sexist stereotype, so I gather, is that girls want to be married by 28, boys more like 32 (where those precise numbers came from, I have no idea). But if for a moment we are to entertain the idea that this stereotype has some kind of grounding in truth, what this would mean for girls is that they are likely to end up accepting the next reasonable marriage proposal they get earlier than boys. Boys, on the other hand, are content to plug away at their careers, playing the field, while spending more time thinking about their cars and lowering their golf handicaps than tying the knot.

These tendencies are said to be at their most bare-faced at weddings where single girls, all of a marriageable age, congregate in one place and naturally only have one thing on their mind: when am *I* going to meet Mr Right? The perfect cocktail of romance, booze, and drunken dancing mean that boys barely need to open their mouths before they are in a girl's cross-hairs.

I had the opportunity to see whether the stories were true for myself when I was invited up to Edinburgh by an old friend of mine, Charlie. His 30-year-old brother was getting married, and a gang of us were going. We drove up the A1, swigging beers in the back, and singing our hearts out to Alanis Morisette's 'Ironic'.

Charlie turned down the music as we passed the 'Edinburgh 8' sign.

'So, boys. Here's the plan. I've been briefed by my brother and there are basically shedloads of the bride's old schoolfriends going tonight – nearly all of them single and gagging for it. So if we don't clear up,[7] we're just going to have to tear it up.'[8]

We roared with approval. For most of us, me included, this was the first proper wedding that we'd been to. By 'proper' I mean that we weren't eight years old and dressed like toy-soldiers, having our faces scrubbed with granny's spit and being told to go to bed by the grown-ups at 9.30 because we were tired/showing-off (read: please leave us alone so we can get pissed). No, tonight was ours for the taking. We would be the last ones to bed, drink the most champagne, and, if Charlie's brother's briefing was to be believed, get the most action.

We turned up at the post-reception dinner half an hour late. The service and reception had been and gone; clearly we had got a bit carried away with that 'swift' half-pint beforehand. We could tell after one quick sweep of the room that at least the first part of the groom's briefing was true; there were a lot of very nicely turned-out girls

---

7 Behaving inappropriately, and getting lucky in the process.
8 Behaving inappropriately.

here. An array of slinky backless dresses and fancy hair-dos filled practically every other seat. Meanwhile, the men were already getting stuck into the claret, snorting away at what a shame it was to have lost another man to 'the other side'.

I found my seat, and slotted right in between two rather lovely looking girls, Eliza and Lucy.

'Ah, so you're the mystery student,' Eliza said. 'We thought that you were going to stand us up.'

'Hi,' I said, sheepishly. 'I'm Will.'

'Well it's nice to meet you. Now come on then, Will, drink this,' Lucy said, putting a glass of wine in my hand, 'you've got some catching up to do.'

After attacking a crate of Fosters with the boys in the car and tequila shots in the hotel bar, this wasn't exactly true. But these girls were clearly up for a bit of fun, and as my student status apparently meant that I had been appointed table jester, I downed the glass.

I learnt pretty quickly that Eliza was already taken. She kept anxiously glancing over her shoulder. I was beginning to sense that my conversation wasn't living up to expectations, so I grabbed her attention the next time she did it.

'Excuse me for asking, but what is it that you're looking at when you turn around like that?'

'Oh it's nothing. It's just my boyfriend. He can act like a real arsehole sometimes at parties. He flirts with other girls and makes a tit of himself like I'm not even there.'

'And you let him get away with it?'

'Well, you know, boys will be boys. I don't want to come across as a total control freak, so I just let him have a good time.'

'That's ridiculous. The girlfriends I have had would never have let me get away with that.'

'Yes, well, you're a lot younger that me – you'll find that girls get better at putting up with shit like that the older they get.'

Aside from the increasingly heavy conversation with Eliza, things were kicking off with Lucy. I don't think I've known anything like it. She was laughing at everything I said, and looked at me as if I was the long lost man in her life, saying, 'Yes, that's so interesting' to just about any semi-serious comment I made. Were all 28-year-old girls always this interested in boys?

After 45 ego-inflating minutes, the boys and I met in the gents' for an update. Judging by the looks on all of our faces, we were very much sticking to plan 'clear up'. Freddie got things going.

'I can't believe it's really true. There is something about girls at weddings – it's like they're on heat or something. The girl next to me was stroking my leg before we'd even got on to the main course!'

Charlie had the biggest grin of all.

'What are you looking so smug about, Charlie?' I asked.

'Let's just say that the sheets in the linen cupboard aren't as pristinely folded as they were.'

Charlie, being the groom's younger brother, was a natural target for the girls. It turned out that one of his brother's old flatmates had always fancied him, and she had seized the first opportunity to do something about it before he had even had the chance to spread the butter on his bread roll.

The night ran on much like any other wedding. The champagne kept coming, the bride and groom left before things got really messy, and the cheese board, having started the night as a beautiful selection of wheels and wedges, was now more like an artist's palate smeared with blues and creamy yellows.

I woke up the next morning in a hotel bedroom somewhere in Leith, with hazy recollections of being bundled into the back of a taxi by Lucy in the small hours of the morning. I made my excuses, something about having to get a train back down south, and managed, by some miracle, to find a bus taking me back into the city centre. I found a café on George Street for a much needed full Scottish breakfast.[9] It was there that the team, one by one, was reunited, each one of us still in our dinner jackets and unbuttoned shirts.

We looked at each other bleary-eyed, having come from all corners of Midlothian, practically speechless. We didn't really know what had hit us. It was like we had been transported into another world, one where getting with a girl wasn't a matter of mustering the courage to talk to them for most of the night, or just grinding up to them from behind on the dance floor, hoping for some kind of positive response. The world of 28 – 30-year-olds was different, at weddings at least. Single girls weren't completely unobtainable, reserved only for the best-looking, most confident boys. They were approachable, friendly and, perhaps most crucially for us boys, up for it. That was a lot more than could be said for the men at

---

9   The addition of black pudding and square sausages being the only apparent differences to an English breakfast.

the party, who seemed pretty content to drink themselves into oblivion, toking hard on their cigars, as if women were the last thing on their minds.

What could explain this shift in girl – boy relations? Perhaps Charlie's brother just had abnormally friendly girl friends, and complete knobs for boy friends. But there appeared to be more of a systematic underlying cause. The thinking behind Flora's marriage proposal at the beginning of this chapter, as well as the experiences of the night, may provide some of the answer.

As I've already mentioned, we all seem to be willing to accept at some point that we aren't going to marry the man or woman of our dreams. Although when we are young and ambitious we convince ourselves that somewhere out there is our perfect partner, and generally want to hold out for as long as possible for that person to come along, might it be that there comes a breaking point at which we realise, unless we get lucky, that in life we have to make compromises, and a choice of wife or husband is no exception? (However utterly depressing that sounds.) If that is indeed the case, it appears that as we near the point where being single is more of a stigma than a life choice, we end up just having to say 'you'll do.'[10]

I tried explaining this to Flora, my future wife (given the fulfilment of certain conditions).

'No, Will, don't be ridiculous. I am not going to just take the next guy that comes along. I've got standards.'

'OK, fair enough. But let me ask you this, if you were

10 As the classic Stephen Stills lyric goes, "There comes a time where if you're not with the one you love, you love the one you're with."

to get married tomorrow, how perfect would the guy have to be?'

'Perfect. He would have to be my dream man.'

'OK, that's what I guessed. I would say the same. Now, imagine that we've fast-forwarded nine years, and you're a single 30-year-old. How perfect would he have to be then?'

'Err, less than perfect.'

'Give me a percentage figure.'

'Sixty percent perfect. As long as he was reasonably good-looking, kind, and had a good job.'

'Exactly – I know you've got standards, but those standards will drop the longer you stay single and want to get married.'

I drew her a graph to prove my point, using Flora as the typical woman:

FIGURE 2: YOU'LL DO HORIZON (woman only)

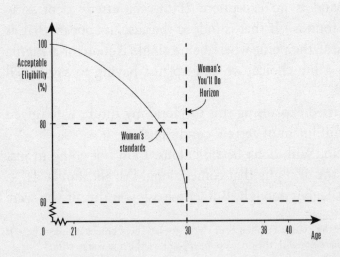

'Acceptable eligibility' is a percentage figure showing how suitable a husband a man has to be for Flora to accept his proposal. This takes in multiple factors that make someone a suitable life partner: looks, intelligence, reliability, wealth, etc. As we can see from the graph, this figure stays high in her early-to-mid twenties, but starts to fall off drastically around the age of 28, the point at which she sees her friends getting married, and the number of good-quality bachelors diminishing. Eventually she'll get to the 'You'll Do Horizon', the point at which she accepts a proposal from the least eligible man she will ever be happy to marry.

It seems the rationale behind this lowering of standards is like a shop having a closing-down sale. Ideally they don't want to start cutting prices too early, as that means less profit, but eventually they have to face the stark reality of closure and sharply cut prices just to get rid of their stock and minimise losses. So, while the shop slashes its prices to increase the number of shoppers who would be willing to pay for their remaining goods, Flora sells herself cheaper too; she changes her perception of who is eligible in order to bring more bachelors into her pool of potential husbands.[11] This is the law of supply and demand at work; the lower the asking price, the more people who are willing to buy the product.

'OK, Will, so what's your point?' Flora asked me,

---

11 Another difference is that Flora would not be willing to marry someone who she is not going to be in some way happy with, whereas a shop would be willing to sell below cost-price in order to minimise their losses. In other words, if she does not get a proposal from someone who meets her minimum acceptable eligibility level, she would rather remain single.

looking unimpressed with my theory so far. 'That all girls are so desperate to get married and have babies that they would be happy to marry a complete loser? And where do men come in? I suppose you're going to say that you have higher standards than women, or something equally as ridiculous and sexist.'

'Well, not exactly. Not in the long run anyway.'

The curve for men works on similar principles, but has one key difference; their 'You'll Do Horizon' lies further to the right than Flora's. This is because, if they are at all like the stereotypical man that I described earlier, they will reach the point in their life where they want to settle down later than Flora. A man's line looks like this:

FIGURE 3: YOU'LL DO HORIZON (man v woman)

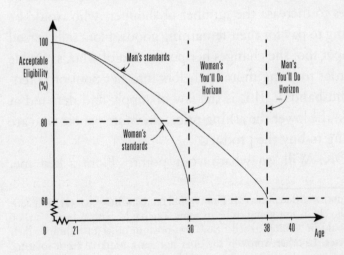

Like Flora, they start off with high standards, but drop them at a slower rate. This is because they, who are not forced to confront the 'You'll Do Horizon' until their late thirties, are willing to hold out for their perfect girl just that bit longer than Flora. They will eventually drop their standards to her level, but this doesn't happen until about six years after she has nested with her perfectly adequate husband.

Another important factor in play is the fact that it is generally more common for a man to marry a woman a lot younger than him than vice versa; few would raise eyebrows at a 34-year-old man marrying a 25-year-old woman, but when it happens the other way around one cannot help but brand it a 'toy boy' marriage. This means that, if Flora and I were to keep our respective levels of acceptable eligibility fixed, the pool of eligible part-ners wouldn't diminish as quickly for me as it would for Flora.

Let me just take stock here. If you accept the, perhaps rather out-dated, assumption that men marry later than women, when it comes to choosing a life-long partner, men can afford to be more patient than women as they have a wider pool of potential partners from which to choose. As we can see from the graph, this results in Flora and my notions of acceptable eligibility diverging over time so that there will come a point where, even though we are both the same age, I will be holding out for an 80 percent woman, but Flora will be making do with a 60 percent man. In other words, a girl marrying a boy her age will have to be more eligible than him if he is going to propose to her.

'OK, Will, I think I've heard enough. You're basically saying that when we're both 30 I'll be on the look out for a safe pair of hands, and you'll still be on the prowl for some slim 25-year-old Oxbridge English graduate with blonde hair, perfect teeth, and a great job.'

'You're right, that doesn't seem like the fairest deal, does it? But not to worry, we've already agreed a marriage deal.'

Flora had a point. Why do men get this deal? Why has society created such blatant double standards so that men can get away with wearing the same suit to every wedding they go to, while girls have to fork out for a new dress each time? Why is it just about acceptable for a man to fart in public whereas it is an abomination for a girl to do the same?[12] Women match, or outperform (allowing for physical differences), men in just about every field of work, sport and the arts. So how have these underlying social norms remained so entrenched?

The answer may lie in men's larger pool of potential spouses which, in economic terms, translates into greater *market power* than women. Market power usually refers to the ability of a company to set prices in a particular market; the greater the market power a company has, the more it will be able to get its way when dealing with other companies and its customers. Take the example of our biggest supermarkets. They are such large purchasers of wholesale foods that they have the power to buy stock at the price and on the terms that they want. For smaller companies,

---

12 I admit these might be not the most poignant of examples of the suffering of women at the hands of their male counterparts, but hopefully you get the point.

a contract with one of these supermarkets means that its product will potentially reach every corner of the UK so is a big deal for them. As the supermarkets know this, they make those smaller companies pay dearly to get on their shelves by buying from them at a discount, and also accepting no financial risk; the supplier only gets paid once the product is bought by a supermarket customer. Here, as supermarkets have a large pool of potential wholesalers from which to buy, if the supplier tries to stand up for itself and insist on a particular price, the supermarket can turn around and simply say, 'Well, we know plenty of other suppliers who would sell for that, so take it or leave it.'

Going back to the example of the closing-down sale, this is an example of a company with *very little* market power. As they are running out of time in which to sell their stock, they have to price their goods to sell to as many customers as possible. There the power lies with the customers, rather than the shop. This is because the shop's planning horizon is a lot shorter than that of its customers; the customers are always going to be shopping on the high street, and are happy to wait as long as is necessary to get a good deal, whereas the company's days are limited, and they must get as much money as possible from their remaining stock in that time. Here the shoe is on the foot of the customer, rather than the company.

In my model, when Flora starts dropping her acceptable eligibility level, I am in the position of the customer, Flora in that of the shop. As she's got less time in which to find a good partner than me, she has to make herself more attractive than I do to attract potential spouses; she drops the price (the acceptable eligibility) at which she is willing to supply her remaining stock (herself).

This greater market power was what I saw the night of Charlie's brother's wedding. Eliza's boyfriend was able to get away with behaving as he did, flirting with other girls and getting inappropriately drunk, whereas she was expected to behave immaculately. If Eliza did try to stand up for herself, her boyfriend could say to her, 'If you can't put up with what I'm doing, I'm sure I can find someone else who can,' just as Tesco can dismiss the pleas of the small supplier.

As I mentioned at the time, this kind of behaviour is something that I could never have expected to get away with with any of *my* girlfriends. But one of the reasons that I have never tried is that in our early twenties girls and boys are in a more equal position; our levels of acceptable eligibility are more or less the same. That means that if I do behave like a knob, my girlfriend can just say, 'I know lots of boys who wouldn't do anything like that; you're dumped.' If Eliza is at all representative of girls her age, however, it appears that as girls approach the You'll Do Horizon, dumping the boy for bad behaviour appears to become decreasingly credible as an option (see more about credible threats in Chapter 12). What this means is that boys have an incentive to behave badly as they know their girlfriends are running out of time to find a husband. They behave like complete arseholes, safe in the knowledge they are unlikely to be dumped, and if they are, there will be plenty of other options available.

I was slightly horrified by how brutal and sexist my analysis was becoming. Surely it couldn't be the case that as soon as we start to approach the You'll Do Horizon all men become utter bastards and women let them get away with it. In fact, looking a little further down the line, when a couple get married you could say that the pendulum of power swings back to the centre, or even tilts in the direction of the girl. If Eliza and her boyfriend did end up getting married, judging by the married couples I know, it wouldn't be unthinkable for there to be an overnight shift in control. He could well wake up the morning after the wedding and find Eliza wearing the trousers he once so complacently wore, and find his social diary, holiday plans, and a list of domestic chores being dictated to him.

The unfair deal between men and women that appears to operate in our late twenties and early thirties therefore only appears to be a small part of the picture. Women get payback for putting up with men's dominance before marriage by getting to pull the strings when they are married; they accept short-term costs in their late twenties in order to get a long-term stream of benefits from marriage onwards. Or, to look at it another way, women submit in the short-term in exchange for a greater share of control in the relationship in the long term; something that has been referred to, in proper books, as the *patriarchal bargain*.[13]

Girls may therefore appear content to put up with boys misbehaving and generally put more effort into their appearance, but this is not necessarily innate behaviour.

---

13 In her paper, *Bargaining with Patriarchy*, Deniz Kandiyoti compares different strategies adopted by women to maximize security and life options when living in patriarchal societies, such as sub-Sarahan Africa. Exercising influence through their husbands and sons is one such strategy.

They may just be great strategic thinkers; they adapt their strategy on how to get a husband, have children, *and* enjoy greater long-term autonomy and control to accommodate the fact that their clock ticks faster than it does for men. This makes perfect sense: when we're in a hurry to get something we want, we are more willing to make compromises, particularly if that means that we will get our own way in the long term. Meanwhile men seem content to surround themselves with nice, pretty, forgiving girls in their late twenties, and then cede control to their wives in marriage.

As I was only in my early twenties, I did not have the chance to put my theory to the test. So I really had no way of knowing if my bedroom-theorising might be a universal law or whether my experience at Charlie's brother's wedding was a one-off. In my own story I was going to have to make do with the fact that girls can be seriously picky, and accept that I needed to up my game if I was going to enjoy anything like the success that I got a little taster for on that crazy night in Edinburgh.

Chapter 6

The Wine Bluffer's Dilemma:

Game Theory

I know that I am not alone in saying that I find wine lists slightly intimidating. I scan the list, which may as well be written in Greek, and don't really take any of it in beyond the extortionate prices that I am expected to pay for something I don't even like that much. Half of me feels like saying to the waiter, 'Chayt-own-uff du Payp – £45? I take it that comes with free refills?'

But when I am on a date I am eager to impress the girl with my supposedly sophisticated tastes, so I try to make my choice appear as considered and knowledgeable as possible. Usually this involves a thoughtful, yet brief (too long and you clearly don't know your stuff), survey of the wine list, and then snapping it shut, apparently resolute and confident in my decision.

On this particular occasion I was with Amber, a girl Flora had set me up with a couple of weeks before. Our first date had gone extraordinarily well. We had similar interests, tastes, and had a few friends in common. I even managed to get a snog at the end of it. Not wanting to blow it, for the second date I decided to play it safe and took her to Sophie's Steakhouse in Covent Garden. It was a chain restaurant, but didn't really feel like one, and it wasn't Pizza Express or Wagamamas: a win-win choice basically.

But things didn't start well. It was late September, when it starts to get *a bit* chilly in the evenings. I stress *a bit* chilly because that is exactly what it is. Think 'this isn't warm' rather than 'my God it's cold'. But for some reason pubs like to respond to the first sign of a drop in temperature by turning up their heating full-blast, and I, an abnormally warm-blooded male, am made to suffer as a result.

I was running late, so had a bit of a march on getting to the tube. I had also been for a quick gym session beforehand, just to make sure that the endorphins would boost my form for the date, and to generally tighten things up. I am a bit paranoid about turning up to dates sweaty, so I walked down the street with my jacket off and shirt half unbuttoned to bring down my body temperature as much as possible. I paused outside the pub where I was meeting Amber, just to check that I wouldn't break into a sweat as soon as I walked in. My heart rate was down, and the breeze was doing a good job of wicking away the sweat on my brow. I was ready. I buttoned up my shirt, put on my jacket, and went for it.

'Oh shit, she's already here,' I thought as I walked anxiously towards her at the bar. Usually I like a few minutes to assess the environment, find a good table, and go to the gents' to sharpen up (or, in fact, to cool down).

But her punctuality – damn her – meant that I just had to wing it.

She looked really pretty, which put my heart rate on the rise again. I kissed her on both cheeks, trying to make the most of my unsweaty face while it lasted. We made small talk and got a couple of drinks in. But then it started. My body turned on the sprinklers – full blast. The first bead ran all the way down my forehead, round the corner of my eye, across my cheek, before the surface tension of my jawline pulled it sharply towards the end of my chin, where it tantalisingly hung for a second or two, before finally dropping to the ground.

I did nothing. I always remembered the lesson I had learnt from my ex-army Geography teacher at school who never let us take our jackets off in lessons, even if it was the hottest June on record outside. 'Just keep as still as you can, boys. Don't try fanning yourselves. It will only make you hotter,' he used to say as the pungent smell of sweaty adolescents filled the room.

I took his lesson to heart and remained perfectly motionless, letting a small reservoir of sweat form neatly on my forehead. Although she might find my sweatiness unattractive, I thought, she must surely admire my ability to handle awkward situations. Finally I made the obvious suggestion:

'Shall we move outside? We may as well make the most of these long evenings while they last.'

'Yes, let's,' Amber said, far too polite, or perhaps gobsmacked, to comment on the blatantly made-up reason for my suggestion.

Once we had finished our drinks and I had, more or

less, managed to dry off (apart from the wet patch on my shirt that was still sticking to my back, which meant that I was now committed to wearing the jacket all evening), we headed towards the restaurant.

An implausibly handsome waiter seated us. He must have been a model. He had dark hair, blue eyes, tanned skin, chiselled jawline, and a triangular torso bulging from beneath his standard-issue black t-shirt (which was probably a size too small for him if you ask me). Just my luck. If the Niagara Falls exhibition wasn't enough to put her off me, now this guy made me look like someone Amber had just picked up off the street. He gave us a couple of menus and the dreaded wine list.

He perched himself on the table next to us, putting his crotch uncomfortably close to my face.

'If I may tell you about a couple of my personal favourites from the menu.'

His good looks had already made matters desperate; now he got me by the balls with his South African accent.

'You should really try the special to start with – baked ricotta cheese and spinach, with flat bread to dip. I tried it myself just now– it's absolutely ace.'

'Ooh that sounds lovely,' said Amber.

'Thanks very much, I'll bear that in mind,' I said, trying to get some control of the situation.

'OK, guys, I'll come back in a sec to grab your orders.'

Amber tried to stop herself from staring at his perfectly formed backside as he left us to serve another table. She was blushing. Who could blame her? He was a beautiful human being. Which left the score, after five minutes, at South African-model-waiter one, sweaty economics student nil.

I needed an equaliser. Come on, Will. It's time to perform. You date, this is what you do. He's just a waiter.

'So shall we go for a bottle of red?'

'Definitely – but I don't really know anything about wine. You choose.'

I homed in on the list. One thing was for sure – I wasn't going to settle for the house red, the cheapest on the menu. I had a date who was apparently more interested in the man who was serving the food than the sweat-dump she'd be eating it with, so I needed something a little flashier than that. The second cheapest was the obvious upgrade, but I'd heard from a number of sources that restaurants are on to guys like me, the ones who know nothing about wine.

What I've heard (from a friend who has a friend in the wine business), is that because we, the wine bluffers, don't want to look cheap, but also don't want to spend more than about £15, we tend to go for the second cheapest bottle, hoping that our willingness to spend an extra £2 will be the difference between looking like someone who just wants something to wash down their steak, and someone who appreciates a bouquet of flavours to swirl in their glass. This effort to mask our ignorance gives the restaurant a clear incentive to put a crap bottle second from top and make a massive mark-up on it; a perfectly laid wine-bluffer's trap.

But I am cleverer than the restaurant gives me credit for. I may not know a lot about wine, but I am an economist.

In response to the restaurant's effort to try and screw me on the second cheapest bottle, I decide to go for the third cheapest. Stick that in your pipe and smoke it, Mr Hunky South African.

The waiter strolled over back to our table.

'So have you guys made up your minds?'

'We sure have. Can we have some calamari to start and then …'

'You're not going for the ricotta and spinach dip I recommended?' he butted in.

I couldn't quite believe that I was being made to justify my decision to the waiter, but did anyway. 'To be honest, we thought that sounded a little heavy for a starter. Don't take it personally.'

He rolled his eyes.

'OK, how about main courses?'

'I'll have the rump steak please, rare.'

'Rump steak? You're sure? There are better steaks on the menu.'

There are also more expensive steaks on the menu, I thought, but came back with, 'I actually really like a rump – the marbling in the centre gives it great flavour.'

'Whatever you say, boss,' he said, not even trying to mask his contempt. 'And what will the lovely lady be having?'

'A sirloin steak please, medium-rare.'

'Excellent choice, if I may say so,' he said. 'And what can I get you guys to drink?'

'We'll have a bottle of the Rio-gia.'

'You mean *Rioka*. Sure, good choice, buddy.'

He had landed a killer blow. I couldn't be bothered to

keep the score any longer.

Amber could sense the tension mounting and came in with a great save. 'Oh how silly of us – I always thought it was pronounced like that too!'

The ordeal of ordering the food and wine had left me slightly shaken, and I found it difficult to focus on the conversation. As we began going over a few basics, updates in our lives since our last drink, university gossip, etc., for some reason I couldn't help but doubt my wine selection strategy. Had I done the right thing by going for the third cheapest bottle? What if the restaurant had realised that smart-arse economists like me were onto them, and had responded by shunting up the crappy bottle on their wine list from second to third cheapest? What if, to take it a stage further, restaurants actually had *two* wine lists, one that had the crappy bottle as the second cheapest, and the other with it as the third cheapest? Then the restaurant could, depending on whether they thought I would go for the third or second cheapest, give me the list that made sure I got the crappy bottle.

'The last time I went for a steak was two months ago with this guy I met on holiday in France last year ...'

Amber was beginning to talk about ex-boyfriends and previous dates she had been on. Not a good sign. She was losing interest. This only made me doubt my wine selection even more. What if she didn't like the wine I had chosen? That could be another nail in the coffin. Trying not to glaze over, I decided to seek comfort in my favourite topic, game theory, and I began to sketch out the strategic battle lines that were in play when I asked for the Rioja.

I wanted two things from my wine selection: to avoid

looking cheap, and good value for money, both without spending more than £15. The restaurant really only wanted one thing: a big profit margin, but without looking like it was ripping off its customers across the board. If we imagine, like I feared, that restaurants do in fact have two wine lists that put a crap bottle as either the second or third cheapest,[14] then those wine lists, if they showed the price the restaurant paid for it, would look a bit like this:

FIGURE 4: Wine Lists A and B

Wine List A

Wine	Cost Price	Price
House	£6	£13
2nd cheapest (crap)	£6	£14
3rd cheapest	£7	£15

Wine List B

Wine	Cost Price	Price
House	£7	£13
2nd cheapest	£7	£14
3rd cheapest (crap)	£7	£15

As I know nothing about wine, and the only way I know how good a wine is before I drink it is its price, as far as I'm concerned, the more expensive the wine, the better the quality. If the restaurant wasn't trying to make

---

14 I'll admit from the outset that this seems hopelessly hypothetical, but when you're being forced to do something like listen to stories about your date's ex-boyfriends, I find that abstracting from reality can provide a welcome distraction.

a profit and sold the wine for the price at which they bought it, then choosing a bottle would be easy. I would know the more money I spent the better the wine would be. But because the restaurant is trying to make a profit, they charge a price higher than what they bought it for. As wine lists do not say how much the restaurant paid for the wine (unlike those above), only they know how much they bought it for, and so when selling it to wine bluffers like me, only they know how good the wine actually is. This gives the restaurant an opportunity to exploit their informational advantage, and rip off customers like me.

The objective for me is therefore to dodge the crap bottle, and choose the wine that gives me best value for money, or, in other words, the wine on which the restaurant makes the least return. Also, as I have already mentioned, under no circumstances will I consider buying the house wine. Although it's usually a pretty solid option, if you're looking to impress it does look like a bit of a cop-out. Because I am a tight-fisted student, I also don't want to pay more than £15. That means that my two possible wine lists look like Figure 5 (although, of course, I cannot be sure of which one is which, as all I see is the name and price of each wine).

I was getting carried away with the wine selection game. I had completely lost track of what Amber was talking about. Judging by the number of times she said that it was 'literally the most amazing thing in the world,' I think it was something to do with her holiday in Thailand the previous summer. I didn't even know why I was bothering with the strategic rationale behind my wine selection anyway; the Rioja was perfectly nice.

FIGURE 5: Wine Bluffer's Dilemma

Wine List A

Wine	Price
Good	£15
Crap	£14

Wine List B

Wine	Price
Good	£15
Crap	£14

The South African came back over. Here we go again, I thought, what's he going to say now? That I could have made a better choice of restaurant?

'Hey, guys, everything OK with the meal?'

'Yes thanks,' Amber said, 'the food is great.'

'And how about the conversation?'

Amber and I stared at each other, completely lost for words.

'Only kidding, guys! You Brits can take yourselves too seriously sometimes. Anyway, let me know if you want another bottle of the Rioja.'

Why was he so keen to force another bottle upon us? Was it because he was trying to shaft us, as I suspected? Just after we ordered our desserts, chocolate brownie and vanilla ice cream, I felt it was time to get back to the model.

The scenario at the moment is that the waiter has a choice of giving me either list A, where he shafts me on the second cheapest bottle, or list B, where he shafts me on the third cheapest bottle. I then make my choice of wine based on what menu I think he has given me. If I think the waiter has given me wine list A, I will choose the third cheapest bottle to avoid getting shafted on the second cheapest. However, if he is a little more sophisticated than that, and he anticipates that I am going to go for the third cheapest, he will give me wine list B, in which case I would do better by going for the second cheapest bottle as the crap bottle is now the third cheapest.

But what if he has anticipated my anticipation of the menu swap? Do I then revert to the third cheapest? Then what if he knows I am going to do that? Our second-guessing of each other's moves could go on forever. It was nearly time for coffee, so the pressure was on if I was going to determine my optimal wine selection strategy *and* get a snog at the end of the evening.

My wine selection model was beginning to look like a classic *zero-sum game*; if I chose the right bottle, I would get value for money and the restaurant would lose profit, but if I chose the wrong one I would lose value for money and the restaurant would gain profit. There was no outcome that we would both be happy with – there had to be one winner and one loser. The wine bluffer's dilemma was therefore rather similar to a penalty kick in football, albeit a simplified one: I (the penalty taker) have to pick the corner of the goal that the waiter (the goalkeeper) chooses not to dive to. If I shoot towards the empty half of the goal, I score; if the goalkeeper correctly guesses which way I'm going to shoot, it is saved.

What's the best strategy for both players in this situation? I pictured myself in my football kit, taking the last-minute penalty against the South African, with Amber looking on from the side-lines, and thought it through. Clearly, if I think that he is stronger diving to his left than to his right, I am going to aim to his right, as that will give me a higher chance of scoring.

However, if he knows that his right-sided weakness is public knowledge, he'll also know that I'm more likely to shoot to the right, and so will in fact (despite it being his 'weaker' side) choose to dive to the right.

As you'll probably already have gathered, when analysing this game it doesn't take long to start piling up increasingly complex layers of knowledge about the other's intentions: 'but what if the goalkeeper knows that I know he knows that I'm stronger going right … what if I know the goalkeeper knows that I know he knows about me knowing what he thought he knew about what I had known?'

Luckily, game theory has a much neater (and less irritating) solution to this conundrum than trying to account for the best option for each and every degree of knowledge or perceived strength or weakness: the best strategy, quite simply, is to randomize, or make our strategy completely unpredictable.[15] Being unpredictable makes it impossible for the goalkeeper to adapt his strategy to make saving the penalty any more likely. However strong you are going to one side, you're actually more likely to score if you shoot

---

15 Research has shown that the best penalty takers actually do this in practice, shooting in each direction 50 percent of the time.

in both directions with equal probability. Basically, with any luck, you're most likely to score on a regular basis just by flipping a coin rather than playing any mind games with the goalkeeper.

If the waiter was in fact a master game-theorist then my strategy of going for the third cheapest was flawed. He would have anticipated my move, and screwed me over by giving me the list with the crappy bottle as the third cheapest. I should, in hindsight, have just randomised.

Before I let my melancholy fully set in, I realised I was getting carried away again. This was all beginning to feel rather too contrived. I may not have liked the waiter, but that did not mean that he was so determined to screw me over on the wine that he would have a wine list especially for people like me who try and beat the restaurant at their own profit-making game. Restaurants only have one wine list – it would be too expensive and impractical to have one perfectly tailored menu for each individual customer to suit their respective budgets and knowledge of the restaurant's strategy. Restaurants have to settle for one strategy to beat the average customer. The average customer is someone, like me, who is on a budget and is concerned about value for money without knowing anything about wine. But, unlike me, the average customer probably doesn't see wine selection as a strategic minefield.

What this means for me and the restaurant in the wine bluffing game is that if the restaurant doesn't expect the average customer to think strategically about their wine selection, then they would do better on average to put the biggest mark- up on the second cheapest bottle. People like me, who are geeky enough to think these things, would therefore do better to choose the third cheapest. The perfect solution, or *Nash Equilibrium,* isn't necessarily the right solution all the time. What's right depends on *whom* you are up against. I may well have thought that I would be clever to randomise my wine choice, thinking that the waiter would swap menus at random, but in reality the restaurant has chosen its strategy to be the best response to the non-strategically minded customer.

I breathed a sigh of relief as I downed the dregs of our third bottle of Rioja. I had made the right choice after all. The combined aphrodisiac effect of the wine and brownie were beginning to make me feel like I wanted to see more of Amber. I was going to try to take her home.

'Shall we get the bill then?' I suggested, trying desperately not to slur my words.

'Good idea, I better be getting home.'

'I don't suppose there's space in the taxi for one more?'

Amber signalled to the waiter for the bill.

'Mmm, I'm not sure, Will. I'm drunk and I don't want to do anything I'd regret later.'

What could there be to regret? I thought. 'OK, fair enough, it's early days. No point in rushing anything. How about we do something next week?'

'I'm quite busy these next few weeks, with exams coming up and all. But will let you know. Sorry for being boring. Exams just really stress me out. Perhaps call me after they're over?'

The exams weren't for another four weeks. I had been constructively dismissed.

'Sure. Sounds good.'

I walked her to the taxi rank. Before there was even a chance for an awkward kiss-or-not-to-kiss moment to develop, she leant in sharply to give me a kiss on the cheek.

'Thanks for a lovely evening, Will. The food was great.'

Shame about everything else, I thought.

Chapter 7

He Loves Me, He Loves Me Not:

Signalling Preferences Under Uncertainty

In the film *The Invention of Lying*, people cannot help but say exactly what they feel. A man picking up his blind date says as soon as she opens the door, 'I hope this date ends in sex,' to which her immediate reply is 'Not me. I don't find you attractive. Come on in.' In this world, there is no uncertainty. Everyone knows exactly what others think of them, and courtship is a simple, albeit dull, affair where potential couples only exchange views on whether they would make a good genetic match, and the sustainability of their joint financial prospects.

If it were only that simple. Instead, I, and everyone else, insists on communicating in a special code, the governing rule of which is that you cannot, ever, say exactly how you feel. Saying, as I have often thought, 'I think you are absolutely wonderful, I think I am falling in love with you' is strictly forbidden. That would be a gross oversupply, and your price would crash to bargain basement levels. Instead, those all-important first few weeks are completely shrouded in agonising uncertainty, and we rely on actions, or signals, to try to relay how we feel about the other. These signals can range from how many Xs you leave at the end of a text message, through the time of day that you ask to meet a girl, to how long you leave it before you call them after a date.

Shortly after Amber had stopped answering my calls, I found myself immersed once again in this world of over-analysing text messages, planning my next move in intricate detail, and trying to cope with my inherent courtship insecurities which were becoming far more acute since the Lizzie episode. I had met a nice, fun, pretty girl called Sarah who had recently broken up with her boyfriend which left me with a window before the market was informed and she was snapped up again. After weeks of library flirtation, I had finally mustered the courage to ask her out for a drink.

The date went well. Perhaps too well. It was a near-perfect exercise in planned spontaneity. We went for cocktails, apparently in the nearest bar we could find to campus (actually a carefully chosen bar well known for its happy hour), went on a stroll to a wine bar where we shared a great bottle of wine (I had the exact bottle in mind a week in advance), and then headed to Soho to try our luck finding some mid-week clubbing (following *Time Out*'s recommendation for Wednesday nights). It all ended perfectly after a walk through Hyde Park with a long, slightly drunken, kiss.

How on earth was I supposed to follow that one up? I sent her a message saying that I had had a good time and would like to meet up again. 'Yeah, sure, sounds good,' she said. I could already tell she was playing this one cool. I learnt from our mutual friends that she had no intention of getting into a relationship and I shouldn't expect too much from her beyond kissing for quite some time. OK, I thought, I know this game. Be cool, establish a monopoly, restrict your supply. Now don't screw it up.

I liked Sarah. I found her attractive, and there was definitely some long-term potential. How was I supposed to communicate this to her without actually saying it? How could I make sure she knew that I was not in it, like many guys in my situation, to get her into bed in as short a time as possible? Saying exactly what my intentions were was clearly not an option. No, I wasn't going to make that mistake again. I was going to have to rely on my actions, or signals, alone. The question was what were the right signals to make.

If we were to return to the world where lying has not yet been invented, there would be no uncertainty which would cut out the need for any signalling at all. I would just say to her 'I would like to spend some more time with you because I think you are fun and attractive, and would also like to sleep with you in due course, but I don't think we have a serious future together' to which she might reply 'I agree, let's spend more time with each other, and I would also like to sleep with you at some point' or 'No thank you. I think you're nice but I do not find you attractive enough to sleep with.' That would save a lot of time agonising over why she still hadn't replied to my text suggesting we should meet up again, two days after I sent it.

Unfortunately, we don't live in this world. People lie. Especially boys who want to sleep with girls, who have developed lying into quite an art form. People can tell lies because talk is cheap. That means a guy, who has no intention of sticking around after he has slept with a girl, can say pretty much whatever he likes if it's going to get the girl into bed, as girls won't have an opportunity to discover that he was lying and punish him for it. In other words, he incurs no cost from telling the lie. Telling lies isn't cheap, however, if you're in a long-term relationship, where they are more likely to be unravelled. One lie usually has to be covered up with another, they become more elaborate and interwoven, and when the liar is finally uncovered, he suffers the consequences of a damaged reputation and the guilt of having broken a girl's heart. In a dating situation such deterrents do not yet exist, and words alone should therefore be taken with a pinch, or two, of salt.

Girls know this. Most of them know by the time they're at their first dance that boys aren't to be trusted. So nice guys have a bit of a problem on their hands. In the early days after meeting someone they like, they have to distinguish themselves from those who have shallower motives. It looks like we have an economic model to work with.

Imagine a simplified world where boys can be divided into two types: sweethearts and dickheads. Sweethearts like to treat girls well, make them happy, and are generally in it for the long term. Dickheads are different from sweethearts in that they are more concerned about how quickly they can add another notch to their bedpost than with a girl's feelings. So, to put it a little more precisely, sweethearts are more patient than dickheads, meaning they value future pay-offs more than instant gratification, and they are made happier by, or derive utility from, the happiness of others (they are said to have *other-regarding preferences*). I think it would be a fair assumption that girls generally prefer sweethearts to dickheads (if that isn't the case, then God help me). But, the problem is, they are completely unable to tell a dickhead apart from a sweetheart based on appearances alone. By the time they know a guy is a dickhead, it's already too late.

In a world of no lying (i.e. where there is no uncertainty) sweethearts would say 'I am a sweetheart' and dickheads would say 'I am a dickhead', and, as girls prefer sweethearts, dickheads would go home empty-handed every night. Once we make the model more realistic, however, and allow lying, dickheads, knowing that girls prefer sweethearts, will try and behave just like a sweetheart by misrepresenting their preferences. Girls, however, know that dickheads have this incentive, so from their perspective there's every chance that a sweetheart, however sincerely he declares his feelings for the girl, is just a dickhead who is very good at putting on a performance to get some action. In this situation words are no longer an effective means of conveying information about one's preferences, so the sweetheart must rely on his actions to reveal his true motives.

Before going further with our dickhead — sweetheart model, it is worth explaining a little more about what signalling is and how it works. A signal is a visible cost incurred by an individual that reveals information about their preferences or what type of person they are, where those preferences or that type would otherwise be uncertain. In what is known as a signalling game, there are two players, a signaller (the one incurring the cost), and a receiver (the one trying to work out the other's preferences or type).

To take an example, imagine that there are two twins, Bill and Ben, and both are applying for a new job working at their local flower-pot factory. Although they are practically identical in every way, Bill is a studious, talented, and dedicated flower-pot maker, whereas Ben is a layabout. Obviously, when it comes to negotiating their contracts, Bill is not going to be terribly happy if he gets paid the same as his brother, as, on a good day, Ben can only make a third of the number of pots Bill makes. The problem for Bill is that the flower-pot factory owner will be completely unable to tell the difference between them when he sets their salaries. As far as he knows, as they look the same and both came across really well at the interview stage, they're both as good as each other. Paying them the same wage is therefore the optimal solution, even though his preferred policy is to pay good workers higher wages to incentivise them to stay at his factory.[16]

Obviously, this will infuriate Bill. He knows he's much better at his job than his brother, but, unless he

---

16 This example is based on Michael Spence's seminal work on signalling theory, 'Job-Market Signaling'.

can do something to change things, he's just going to have to suck up the fact that he will be on the same wage as him, at least to begin with. To secure a higher wage from the outset, Bill will therefore have to distinguish himself from his brother. As appearances alone are not enough, Bill will have to adopt the role of a signaller to do this: he will have to accept a cost that Ben would not be willing to incur, so that the factory owner (the receiver) is able to tell them apart. Exactly what type of cost might Bill have to accept to distinguish himself from his inferior pot-making sibling?

One such type-revealing cost is to have a university degree. In the case of Bill and Ben, since the prospect of sitting through hours of lectures and tutorials on flower-pot design and manufacture would be completely unbearable to Ben, while it would actually be rather exciting for Bill, accepting the costs associated with a university degree, namely time and effort, would be something that only Bill would be willing to do. Ben, on the other hand, would be better off taking a lower paid job at a less prestigious flower-pot factory without getting a degree. Therefore the factory owner, the receiver, can take a degree as a reliable, or credible, signal that Bill is a good worker, and pay him accordingly.[17]

Imagine now that a new university, The Institute for Flower Pottery, has just started a degree programme that involves half the amount of work to graduate than the more traditional courses. Most of it can be done online in the comfort of your own home, and there's no written

---

17 In Spence's model he assumes, for simplicity, that a university degree does not improve a worker's ability.

exam. In fact, the degree is so easy to get that even Ben will be happy to do it. The consequences of this are that, as both Bill and Ben are now willing to get one, a degree becomes an ineffective, or 'noisy,' signal, and no longer distinguishes the good workers (like Bill) from the bad workers (like Ben). The factory owner will then be back where he started, and pay both of them the same wage. Bill will therefore be forced to incur extra costs, such as a post-graduate degree in advanced flower pottery, in order to signal to the factory owner that he deserves a bigger pay packet.

What might our sweethearts be able to learn from Bill? It would appear that the key for the sweethearts is to find a particular type of cost that only they are willing to accept, one that a dickhead would find intolerable. Taking a girl out for dinner is usually seen as a pretty safe bet if you want to show her that you're interested. Nonetheless, however much you spend, this is not going to be the type-revealing cost that we're looking for. Sweethearts and dickheads are just as likely to take a girl out to dinner, only dickheads see it as a prelude to a cab home to their apartment, and sweethearts see it as laying the foundations for a relationship. A sweetheart could take a girl out to a Michelin-star restaurant to show how much he cared for the girl, but a dickhead could take them to the same restaurant if he wanted sex that badly. Although the gesture of taking the girl out is made with entirely different motives, they look the same to the girl; they are *observationally equivalent*, and so no clear information is relayed about the sweetheart's preferences. It is a noisy signal.

What I have said here so far about taking girls out for

dinner touches on a modern offspring from the age-old dilemma of whether a boy should pay for a girl's dinner on a first date: when you've offered to take a girl on a date, is it acceptable to use restaurant vouchers to pay for the bill? One of my friends, James, has always been of the opinion that it is acceptable, as long as you make it clear from the outset that's what's going to happen. He would say 'I've got these vouchers for this nice new restaurant – I don't suppose you fancy joining me to try it out?' Awkwardly revealing a folded, crumpled print-out when it comes to paying the bill, on the other hand, is rather cringe-making. He has often tried to persuade me that the date should be about good food and conversation, not how much it costs. If after dinner the girl thinks, 'That was a good date, but the fact he paid half price for it means James is a cheapskate and I'm frankly not interested,' that reveals quite a lot about her own preferences. She'd rather James had paid double the price even though she received nothing extra for herself in return. In other words, she would be gaining utility from James' disutility. James's technical term for this character type is 'spiteful wench.'

As you might imagine, James's view has not exactly had a sympathetic reception from various girls we both know. One girl I spoke to said, 'How do you think that makes the girl feel if you only want to take them out because you are getting half-price? It makes us feel cheap, like we're not worth it. And anyway I find the fact that you all seem to assume you should pay the bill, just because you're the man, frankly rather insulting.'

'OK,' I say in James's defence, putting on my worst

kind of economist's (look at me, I'm so clever) voice, 'how would you feel if at the end of a date I whipped out a card that does not halve the price of the meal, but doubles it instead? Would that make you feel like I value you twice as much?'

'No', she said, 'that would just make me think that you are a wanker.'

Fair enough. That would be a pretty wankerish thing to do. You may as well use a £20 note to light her cigarette. But how does this finding fit into our signalling model? Clearly, what you pay does bear some relevance to your preferences when it comes to signalling, but only if you are visibly paying below the normal price. An unwillingness to pay for dinner is the equivalent of Bill choosing not to go to university; it inadvertently signals that you're a type of person which you are not. To avoid this risk, James's suggestion was this: if you are going to use vouchers, do it on the sly and make sure you arrange it with the restaurant in advance. Not very sweetheart – in fact well into dickhead territory – but I can see where he is coming from.

The voucher debate aside, we need to go back to our original assumptions about sweethearts and dickheads to work out exactly what is required for the sweetheart to stand out from his less honourable contemporaries.

Sweethearts are patient, which means they don't mind taking their time thinking about a girl and how best to make her happy. They are content to wait for their pay-off. Dickheads, meanwhile, are impatient, so do not value pay-offs as much if they have put a lot of time into getting them. They'd rather spend the time that the sweetheart puts into planning a date into something else, like hunting down their next one-night stand. This appears to be the difference the sweetheart needs to exploit. The type-revealing cost, or signal, that the sweetheart needs to incur could therefore be, quite simply, time. That is to say, time either thinking about how to make a girl happy, or time spent with her before developing a relationship any further. Going back to the example of taking a girl to a restaurant, we've already established that spending money in itself is no way to reveal one's preferences. Instead, a carefully considered choice of restaurant, perhaps one that shows some kind of link to something you discussed at your last meeting, would, in theory, be much more effective as a signal of genuine interest. For example, if she has expressed a fondness for the Middle East, a simple Lebanese mezze would go a lot further than a fancy French restaurant.

There is a whole range of different signals that one can give off to convey patience. One is choosing a lunch date rather than a dinner date. Lunch dates do not flow as naturally into the bedroom as dinner dates. An invitation to lunch says 'I have no intention of trying it on with you, this time.' An invitation to dinner says 'If this goes to plan, I'll be inviting you around to mine for coffee afterwards.' Similarly, by arranging to meet a girl as part of a group, like having them around for dinner with a group of friends, you are already inhibiting your chances of anything happening on that particular occasion. It gives off an entirely non-predatory, or patient, signal. One-on-one dinner dates, on the other hand, whilst they can be enjoyable, intimate affairs, can make one come across as a hunter cornering his prey. It can convey impatience, or taking the path of least resistance from dining table to bedroom.

Going back briefly to the lessons I learnt in Chapter 1, evidence of too much planning, accepting too high a cost, could be an oversupply. Or, to put it another way, it can be just plain creepy. It can make you look like an obsessive, or like someone who simply has nothing else better to do (re-reading what I have written at the start of this chapter indicates that I may fall into this category occasionally). So, you need a costly signal that can convey information about your preferences without diminishing your market value. I got to work thinking about how I would follow up my first date keeping this trade-off in mind.

It was going to be a lunch date, in the park. I had kissed Sarah the last time I had seen her. Kissing in a public place, in broad daylight, would be a lot harder. I would have to wait for that. We'd go and pick up a sandwich from the local deli, and laze around on the grass, chatting. The plan was meant to signal that I was happy to put the brakes on, as well as show I was interested for more. Now I just had to ask her.

Sarah said that sounded great, but couldn't make it on the day I first suggested, or on my second suggestion, and didn't offer any alternative dates when she would be free, ever. It is always a bit of a head screw when a girl does that. You suddenly feel totally helpless. It is not an outright rejection, but far from a resounding yes. Do you go through an entire calendar month ascertaining by a process of elimination when she is next available, basically making it sound like you have freed up your entire diary just for her?[18] Or do you put the ball in her court and say just let me know when you want to do something, which sounds equally pathetic, and is an offer that can be easily ignored. Instead I opted for a rather defeatist approach by sending a 'well, have a lovely time and I hope to see you soon' sort of message. She didn't reply.

---

18 This would also drastically undermine your bargaining power in the situation, something I discuss in Chapter 9.

Chapter 8

The Hugh Grant Paradox:

Signalling Preferences Under Uncertainty (Part Two)

I needed to find another way into Sarah's heart. My 'sweetheart' theory clearly hadn't quite done the trick. Perhaps being Mr Nice Guy all the time wasn't always what a girl wanted after all. It looked as if I needed another signal. I needed a girl's opinion, and there was only one person who came to mind.

'Flora, what do you look for in a man?'

'Oh God. William, who is it this time?'

'I've met this amazing girl Sarah, she's super-hot, really nice but quite hard to pin down. Definitely not a complete mental case like the last one. I've asked her out on a second date.'

'And did she say yes?'

'Not exactly. But she didn't say no either.'

'And how can I help exactly?'

'I just want to know what line to take. What do

girls like? I've tried nice, but that doesn't seem to have worked.'

'Girls like a guy with confidence.'

'Is that it? Confidence?'

'Well obviously not only that. But it's a good starting point. It will grab her attention. It's a lot easier for a girl to resist a guy with good looks than one with confidence.'

'Right, so what do I do?'

'I don't have all the answers, Will. Just be yourself, be self-assured. Don't dither. Go and get her! Oh, and whatever you do, don't be arrogant.'

Flora's advice appeared to go to the heart of the matter. Sending texts along the lines of 'hope to see you soon' didn't exactly display much self-belief, so no wonder she didn't reply. But what was it that made confidence so attractive? Was it attractive in itself, or was it signalling some other quality? And, more importantly, how could I show confidence without spilling over into arrogance?

One thing was clear from Flora's advice: girls find confidence in a man attractive but arrogance a complete turn off. Even though confidence and arrogance can be seen as being on a single scale of self-assuredness, they can have drastically different consequences; show confidence and the girls will see you as a leader among men; be *too* confident, however, and they'll see you as an arrogant prick. How are we supposed to know where to draw the line? Even if we thought we knew the answer to this, some girls might disagree; while one girl might find a guy irresistibly confident, another might find him repulsively arrogant. It looked as though I had an impossible balancing act on my hands. But then I had an idea – I started to analyse the problem by asking what might first attract a girl to a boy at a flat party, where everyone was meeting for the first time, and there has been a power cut so looks are completely taken out of the equation.

I am going to start off my analysis with an assumption: girls find boys who are good at things, whether it be music, sport, or brainwork, more attractive than those who are not, all other things being equal. Hopefully this shouldn't be too controversial (I certainly find girls who are good at things more attractive than incompetent ones). In a flat party situation, however, it can be pretty difficult to show off one's abilities to the opposite sex (unless your particular talent happens to be dancing, which mine definitely isn't). Instead, we can only give off impressions of our abilities, either by talking about them, or by giving off a general air that we will go on to achieve things in life. Rather like the situation with the sweethearts and dickheads, at a flat party we are therefore in an environment of imperfect information, where only the signaller knows what type of person he is, and he has to rely on signals to show what type of person he is to the receivers.

In such a situation, it seems that confidence is attractive because it suggests to those around you that you are pretty good at whatever you do. By speaking knowledgeably and self-assuredly, and having a general purposive air about you, the chances are people will think you know what you're doing, and that your life is going somewhere, even though they have no idea of how capable a person you actually are. Being reserved, hesitant, and disengaged, on the other hand, will suggest the opposite, even if you are in fact supremely talented, and are bound for fame and fortune. As you can see, if we have no way of confirming or refuting our first impressions of his ability, a boy's *actual* ability has very little or no impact on how attractive he'll be to a girl. Instead it's only his stated, or apparent, ability that counts.

Things get more complicated when we put arrogance in the mix. Arrogance is an overstated expression of one's own abilities. Usually it is interpreted not as a sign of underlying ability, but as a defence mechanism used to try and quash any lingering suspicions of incompetence. But in this flat party scenario, where it isn't possible to tell whether a person is in fact exaggerating these abilities, there will always be a danger that a confident person will come across as arrogant (and therefore unattractive), and an arrogant person might be seen as confident (and therefore attractive).

As a result, self-assuredness can be interpreted as being either confident or arrogant, even though the underlying quality of the person giving those signals is completely different. Similar to what I described with taking a girl out on a date, this ambiguity makes it a *noisy signal*. How then can a confident person, knowing that his confidence is attractive to girls, but that showing it might be interpreted as arrogance, signal his quality?

I put this past Freddie. I was sure I could pick up a few tips from the master of the five-minute pick up.

'You've just got to tell a few jokes at your own expense – girls love that.'

'Er, go on.'

'You know, make fun of yourself, show a few weaknesses. Girls love a strong, confident man, but they won't

be as drawn to you if they don't think they have anything
to work on, something they can improve in you.'

'So what about something like, "I'm really rubbish at
talking to girls" – would that work?'

'Will, no, you're missing the point. Girls love something to work on, but not something as fundamental as
that. They're looking for a boyfriend, not a charity case.'

'Not something too fundamental? What, then?'

'I suppose you want me to sleep with this girl too, after
I've chatted her up for you?'

'Freddie, seriously, I need some help here.'

'OK, just try telling her an embarrassing story about
yourself. It can be anything, like something from your
childhood.'

'Like the time I was caught peeing in my brother's bath
when he was in it?'

Freddie looked at me like he didn't know whether he
was more disgusted or frustrated.

'I'm sure you'll think of something,' he said, heading
out the door for his 11 o'clock lecture.

I could see now that self-deprecation could well
be the answer to the confident man's problem. A self-
deprecating remark or story draws attention to one's
own shortcomings, or deliberately *understates* one's own
abilities, rather than affirming them. This seems to be
counter-intuitive, as it is abilities, not weaknesses, that

girls generally find attractive. But this might be the whole point. In a crowded room full of confident or arrogant guys, highlighting one's own weaknesses might be the only way of sending a credible signal that you are a capable person. This is because a self-deprecating remark is itself an act of confidence, as it shows everyone that your underlying reserves of talent and ability are so abundant that you can easily afford to suffer self-inflicted damage to your reputation.[19] Arrogant people, on the other hand, do not enjoy such deep reserves, and so highlighting their own weaknesses is not a cost they are willing to accept. A confident person can make a self-deprecating remark to signal their confidence, and therefore their abilities, without the risk of coming across as arrogant. This is because confidence sends a signal on an entirely different frequency to arrogance, so there is no risk of the two signals being confused. If I was right, then I could well have cracked the Hugh Grant Paradox – why on earth do women find a man with apparently so little self-esteem so irresistible?

The graph opposite illustrates how this works.

This graph shows two variables: expressed ability, which is observable, and actual ability, which is not. The right-hand side of the graph is the one that we're really interested in. In my case, I might sometimes creep into the bottom left-hand quarter (self-loathing) when it came

---

19 If it was money that girls found attractive, not talent or ability, the equivalent signal would be for a man to deliberately wreck, in the style of Pierce Brosnan in *The Thomas Crown Affair*, his $10m yacht in an elaborate stunt. Often the most effective displays of wealth are those which show a complete disregard for money, rather than those that put it to some extravagant use.

FIGURE 6: The Hugh Grant Paradox

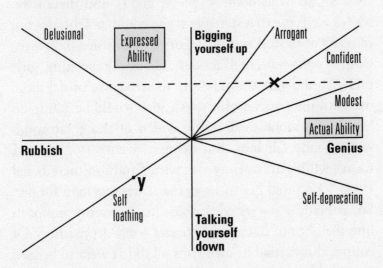

to my abilities with girls, but I certainly wasn't at any risk of being a top-left quarter type of guy (delusional). Turning our attention to the top right-hand quarter, we can see that arrogant people overstate their abilities, they have a steeper line than those who are merely confident, whose expressed ability is roughly proportionate to their actual ability. Modest people are represented by a flatter line, as their actual abilities tend to be greater than they generally like to admit. Finally, someone who is self-deprecating appears in the bottom right quarter as they not only understate their actual abilities, but say they are actually *bad* at that thing, even though they may, in fact, be very good at it.

As illustrated by the dotted line, if only expressed ability is observable, and you express your ability at, say, cooking, to be at point X (pretty good), and there is no way of verifying that statement, you could, potentially, fall into any of the following categories: 1) delusional; 2) arrogant; 3) confident; or 4) modest. Generally speaking, girls prefer confidence and modesty to arrogance or delusion, but with information this sparse girls would be acting on blind faith alone in deciding which of those categories you actually fell into. But being a scientist (of sorts), I wasn't willing to rest my fate with Sarah on mere belief alone – I wanted her to *know* that I was the man for her. So, as Freddie suggested, I needed to move my approach into the bottom right hand quarter – self-deprecation. Of course, this carried its own risks – I didn't want to be seen as a self-loathing no-hoper.[20] To avoid this problem, I was going to have to use a combination of signals – i.e. I had to be confident *and* self-deprecate.

After spending a good couple of hours finalising the graph, I felt that I had finally cracked the puzzle. I called her up that evening, brimming with the type of excitement I usually only got when I was nearing the end of a particularly long equation, and I could see that all the variables, bar one, were going to cancel.

'Sarah, it's Will. How you doing?'

'Will! So nice to hear from you. Sorry I've been totally rubbish getting back to you. It's funny you called, actually, because I was literally just now going to suggest that we got together for that little picnic suggestion of yours.'

---

20 See point *y* on the graph.

I couldn't believe it. I had been planning this call for days now, and she just came straight out, unprompted, with the words I never thought she would say in my wildest dreams – she wanted to see me again. I mentally[21] ripped up the first six pages of the call script, and tried to restore my focus.

'Wow, I mean, yeah sure, that would be great. I was just calling about that. I hadn't heard from you in a while so I just guessed that picnics weren't really your thing.'

'Don't be ridiculous – I love picnics! Where were you thinking?'

'How's Saturday for you in St James's Park?'

'Sounds fab. Meet at one in Trafalgar Square by the lions?'

'Done – see you then.'

'Super – bye!'

The conversation had only lasted about 80 seconds, but it left my heart thumping hard. It really couldn't have gone any better; not only had she said yes, but she actually sounded excited to see me – she wasn't just going through the motions of the second date formalities and saying yes because it would be rude not to. The picnic idea appeared to have gone down a treat – perhaps the 'sweetheart' approach wasn't so flawed after all.

I was in a complete daze the rest of that week. All I could think about was the date. Do I go all out on the picnic and stock up on fancy M&S goodies, or do we just pick up a few bits and pieces from Tesco Express? What do we do after the date? Do I try to kiss her? In the end, to

---

21 I promise I didn't actually write down the script for the call.

avoid the risk of an oversupply, I went for Tesco. And yes, I was going to try to kiss her (why I deliberated so much over that one I just don't know).

I made my way over to Trafalgar Square to meet Sarah, as arranged. I have to admit, I was so nervous I considered popping into a nearby pub for a quick pint to calm me down. As Flora had suggested, I needed to be confident. But I realised beer on the breath at 12.30 might not go down so well, so I just went for it sober. In the end the beer proved to be unnecessary anyway – my nerves evaporated as soon as I saw the warmth of her smile as she stood at the feet of one of the lions.

'And so we meet again,' she said as we went in for a quick hug and kiss on the cheek.

'Yes, it would appear that we have.'[22]

'Will, I'm sorry that it took me so long to get back to you.'

'Don't be silly Sarah, there's no need for that – I'm quite used to people turning down my picnic offers.'

She laughed. Without even intending it (people do actually turn down my picnic offers quite regularly), I had just landed my first self-deprecating line, and it appeared to have worked.

'I'm sure that's not true! Anyway, I'm here now. So where do you want to pick up the goodies?'

I gestured towards the Tesco Express on the other side of the road.

'Perfect! I've always loved a good spread from Tesco's snacks and baked goods section.'

---

22 Really, Will? You can do better than that.

Enthusiastic. Not fussy about food. I liked that about Sarah.

We went into St James's Park laden with a selection of four-for-£1 bread rolls, Philadelphia, wafer-thin ham, two packs of tropical fruit salad, a bottle of Cava, and a pack of ten plastic tumblers. It wasn't exactly a meal fit for a king, but that, somehow, didn't seem to matter – 20 minutes in, the date was going perfectly.

We found a spot beside one of the duck ponds, and sat cross-legged on the grass, contently nibbling at our, admittedly tasteless, hand-made cream cheese and ham rolls. We were sitting about three feet apart – making a kiss, for the time being, only a remote possibility. We chatted away about how things had been since our last (perfectly orchestrated) date, complained about work, and gossiped about our mutual friends. The conversation was pretty light, but for a whole hour we barely broke eye contact – there just didn't seem to be anything else worth looking at, not for me anyway. During the course of that hour, I came to realise just how beautiful Sarah was.

Things were clearly going well. The gap between us was now only two feet (after a few subtle shuffles from me, although I am sure she had also moved in an inch or two), and judging by the increasing flirtiness and giggliness of our conversation, the Cava was going to our heads. But just as I considered moving in an extra couple of inches, to take me well within lunging range, an old problem of mine, one that I used to experience regularly during my school assembly days at junior school, suddenly overcame me; I was getting pins and needles in my left leg. In normal circumstances, I'd just stretch out my leg to resume normal circulatory service. But I was entering a critical phase in the date, and I felt that any sudden movement could be disastrous. So, in defiance of what my body demanded, I remained in the cross-legged position, and shuffled in another inch. I'm sure it will sort itself out, I thought. Before I had any opportunity to put my kissing plan into action, however, Sarah made another suggestion.

'Shall we go for a little stroll through the park then? It would be nice to stretch our legs.'

'Yes absolutely – great plan,' knowing full well what was about to happen.

Sarah leapt to her feet, and held out her hand to help me up. I took it, and started to pull myself up, only for my blood-starved leg to buckle the second the sole of my foot touched the ground. I went crashing back down to earth.

'My God, Will, are you OK?'

Trying my best to conceal my affliction, I quickly thought up an excuse: 'I was thinking, why don't we just stay here? The pond is just so lovely.'

'Will, it's just a pond. Come on. Get up.'

'You're right, give me a second.'

I tried to get back to my feet. While this time I had just about enough blood in my leg to manage standing, walking proved to be too much to ask for – I was effectively crippled. I looked like I had come straight out of a meeting at the Ministry of Silly Walks.

'My God, Will, what on earth is wrong with you?'

'I'm terribly sorry – walking has never really been a strong point for me.'

She laughed. 'You are a funny one. Here, let me help you along.'

She wrapped her arm around my waist, tilting her head against my shoulder. For a moment I wasn't sure whether she was just offering some physical support, or showing me some kind of affection, so I decided not to reciprocate for fear that I had misinterpreted her gesture. To my relief, the stroking of my back gave me the confirmation that I was looking for, so I put my arm around her shoulder. And so there we were, walking arm in arm through St James's Park. It was so obviously the right time to kiss Sarah that I became nervous with anticipation, and then painfully conscious of my every move, and the fact that we hadn't said anything since our arms interlocked behind our backs.

'Parks are great, aren't they?' I finally came up with.

Sarah honoured my non-comment with a polite, but equally inane response; 'Yes, I suppose they are.'

Just as we settled back into our increasingly tantalising silence, it hit me: 'Not exactly my most thought-provoking conversation starter of the day, then.'

Sarah burst into laughter. We stopped walking.

'What is it?' I asked, not sure whether I had taken my self-deprecation technique too far, and made myself the object of ridicule, rather than affection.

'Oh Will, you're so full of rubbish sometimes!'

'Why, what did I say?!'

'I can tell when you want to kiss me because you start splurting complete nonsense.'

'Really, I'm that obvious?'

'Yes! It's adorable.'

'Well, I do want to kiss you, as it so happens.'

'That's lucky because so do I.'

'Thank God for that.'

'Oh William, do be quiet.'

In textbook fashion, Sarah then reached her arms around my neck, I put my arms around her waist, and we kissed.

Some people say it's all about the first kiss, and that's where relationships are made or broken before they even begin. I have to disagree. First kisses are easy – there are no expectations to dash or fulfil, and so, free from that burden, you can usually just go for it, albeit whilst sticking to the less controversial techniques. The second kiss, however, like the difficult second album, knowing how exciting, fresh and new the first one had been, is laden with back-breaking quantities of expectation, and so any irregularity in rhythm, sloppiness, tongue movements, or flavour will be duly noted.

Sarah and my second kiss, though, I am pleased to say, was pretty goddam awesome. Cheers Hugh.

Chapter 9

The Battle of the Diaries:
Bargaining Power

Factoring someone else's plans into my weekly routine came as a bit of a shock. I'd gotten used to doing pretty much whatever I wanted over years of single-hood. I'd worked on the basis that after a first, second, and even third date, you should leave your next planned rendezvous as vague as possible, using classic lines such as 'I'll give you a call' or 'Let's do something soon,' which committed me to seeing them again just about as much as clicking 'attending' on the Facebook invitation did to actually turning up. Each date was a separate event, a set piece, organised with little or no knowledge of the other's diary commitments. That was about to change. It suddenly dawned on me, after another nice evening with Sarah, that after saying our goodbyes we probably should arrange when we were next going to see each other. To leave it open, like normal, just seemed a bit too casual.

'So what are your plans for this weekend?' I asked, hoping she'd reply with something cheesy like, 'Whatever you're doing.'

'Well,' Sarah said, taking in a deep breath (that's never a good sign), 'I am seeing an old friend from school on Friday night. We said ages ago that we'd go and see our friend's play. Then, I know this sounds boring, but I am really behind with work at the moment so need to work on Saturday and Sunday.'

I didn't say anything, still hoping to hear some kind of rider like 'but why don't we do lunch on Sunday?' Instead she said, pitifully, 'Why don't I give you a call?' Ouch. She'd used one of my lines.

I made a pretty lame attempt at levering open a window for me to see her. 'Oh come on Sarah, you can't possibly need to be working all weekend already. Exams are ages away! Why don't we go for a drink on Saturday?'

'Ah, I've got a dinner then. Will, why don't I just call you next week and we'll do something fun?'

Ouch. Line number two.

'OK, cool. I'll speak to you then.'

The next few weeks followed much the same pattern. I had to fight for her time. She gave me narrower and narrower slots when I could see her. It was like I was dating the most popular girl at university; she was at parties practically every night (like most History of Art students), visited her friends at other universities every other weekend, and only saw me for the occasional drink (and, yes, sex, of course – she was quite generous like that). Things felt OK when I was actually with her, but the amount of stuff she was getting up to, without including me, was getting a little ridiculous. My infatuation for her meant I was happy to put up with this treatment for a while; it was all about 'the chase' after all.[23] I just had to think of more imaginative things to do, surprise her, anything to get her attention and put me higher on her list of priorities.

It worked, for a time. I took her on evenings trying out nice little restaurants and pubs, went to gigs and for walks in the park. I really tried to signal how I felt. It was still early days, so talking to her directly about how I felt badly treated wasn't really an option. Having a 'relationship management' chat when we were supposed to be enjoying our honeymoon period could only end in disaster. But this clearly wasn't sustainable. I was constantly on edge, and felt that if I didn't come up with the goods she'd be gone forever by the end of the week. I needed to resort to more drastic measures. It was time to think like an economist.

It was perfectly clear what she was doing. She wanted to show me what a great life she was already having before I even arrived on the scene. She was effectively saying, 'Look at me, I have all these friends, all these interests, what have you got that can make my life any better than it already is?' Or, to put it another way, she was saying that if I didn't accede to her terms of the relationship (i.e. one where she wears the trousers), she could just walk away and be better off without me. This may sound brutal, but it was working, whether she intended it or not. I saw what a great girl she was, and I had to dig deep to grab her attention.

It appeared that we were in a classic bargaining

---

23 That's what I tried telling myself anyway.

situation: there was a clear opportunity for mutual benefit by us being together, or reaching some kind of 'relationship agreement,' but we both wanted that agreement to favour our own individual benefit more than the other's. Who was going to end up coming out with the better bargain once we settled on the terms of this agreement depended on our respective levels of *bargaining power*, which, among other things, was determined by a) what we could get if we didn't end up agreeing anything – our *outside options*; and b) how happy we were to accept the consequences of failing to reach an agreement – our *risk attitude*. I needed to boost both these sources of bargaining power if I was going to put a stop to Sarah's, so far unchallenged, claim to wearing the trousers of the relationship.

First, I needed to increase my **outside options.**

When we find ourselves in any bargaining situation, we invariably get a better deal if we can point to the offers that we already have on the table from other people. For example, one time when I went for a curry on Brick Lane, where there were hundreds of curry houses competing for my business, I got an offer from Bangalore Dreams for a starter, curry, and a pint of lager for £10. Thinking I could get an even better deal than this, I then went along to the next place, Curry Galore, told them about Bangalore Dreams' deal, and was promptly offered an extra pint at no extra cost. They did this as they knew that, to get my business, they had to give me a better deal than the one I knew I could already get, or they would get nothing.

Here, having an outside option, something that I knew I could get for certain without accepting Curry Galore's offer, clearly increased my bargaining power, and got me a better deal.

With Sarah, I very much felt like the guy from Curry Galore, but I wasn't selling curries. It was me I was trying to get her to buy. She had an immense array of outside options, and I was being forced to give her better offers than her other potential plans to make sure she kept accepting them. I was being taken for a ride, and I needed to do something about it. I had to level the playing field.

I filled my diary, choc-a-block. I arranged to see friends I hadn't seen in years. I went on pub crawls, went to football matches and comedy clubs, the kind of things guys are supposed to do when they are at university. For once it was me who was busier than Sarah, I was the one turning her down. I had increased the number of my outside options, and with it, my bargaining power. We still managed to see each other and enjoyed the other's company, but behind the scenes there was a cold war in full swing; it was a battle of the diaries.

On one occasion, I confess, I took it as far as telling her that the drink I was having had gone on for two hours longer than it actually had just to make me appear busier than I really was. Those two fabricated hours were among the most desperate of my life. I sat there in my flat flicking through TV channels, picking at a ready-made meal, knowing full well that I could be with Sarah if I wasn't so determined not to yield to her power. She gave me a call to see how I was getting on.

'Sarah, hi, how's it going?'

'Good thanks, just been to see the girls for a movie-night in – are you nearly done with your drink?'

God I wanted to say yes. But somehow my rational self said otherwise – not seeing her must be in my long term interest.

'Mmm, really sorry Sarah, but I'm still tied up with the guys. Probably not going to be back for another hour or two.'

'Check you guys out – out till one on a Monday. Shall we meet up tomorrow for lunch then?'

It was actually working – she was fitting her plans around mine.

'Yeah, that works for me. Got a lecture at 1.30[24] so we may have to be quick.'

'OK, cool. I can't wait to see you – it feels like ages since we last properly saw each other.'

However comforting that was to hear, I decided to land another killer blow to crystalise everything I had gained that evening:

'Sarah, really sorry, I've got to go. The guys are giving me a hard time for being on the phone. Talk tomorrow. Night.'

'Night, Will.'

The fact that Sarah hadn't just completely lost interest in me, despite my lack of availability, suggested that she was at least still interested in a relationship. As I had learnt in Chapter 3, it could well have been *because* of my lack

---

24 Another lie.

of availability, rather than in spite of it, that this was the case. But I knew that I was treading a fine line. I couldn't keep this up forever and expect her to put up with it – this strategy was fraught with the risk that she might reach a breaking point and realise I just wasn't worth the trouble – I would have priced myself out. Nonetheless, the by-product to increasing my outside options, my apparent indifference to losing Sarah, was probably another source of my increased bargaining power in the relationship – my apparently greater *risk tolerance* had suddenly given me the upper hand.

It's not hard to relate to why this might be the case. If we give the impression that we're happy to lose everything unless we get our way, that usually gives us the upper hand in negotiations with someone who isn't as gung-ho about the prospect of walking away with nothing. In a poker game, for instance, a player who is generally more willing to risk all his chips on one hand is more likely to win a hand by making his opponents fold than someone who bets more conservatively. Perhaps this is why my earlier assumption that girls prefer sweethearts to dickheads isn't always true – dickheads, who generally show a lack of attachment to a girl, have a remarkable ability to really get a grip of a girl's affections, almost to the point of complete dominance (much to the bewilderment and frustration of so-called sweethearts like myself).

My analysis of the situation, although encouraging insofar as it had brought Sarah more within my grasp, made me feel like a stranger to myself. I couldn't really believe what had got into me. Sarah clearly felt let down, and I chose to do nothing about it. Instead, I had chosen to exploit it for my own gain. Was this really the *Romantic Economist* at work? Or was this just the way these things had to be if I was going to lock Sarah into my life? Alternatively (and this was the reality I most feared), had I just become a dickhead like the rest of them? I needed my inner sweetheart to make a comeback, as much for my own sense of moral wellbeing as for Sarah's feelings. We met up for the lunch we had arranged the day before.

'Hello stranger,' Sarah said as I sat down opposite her in the Picnic Basket, a small sandwich shop just off campus.

'Sarah, hi, how are things?'

'Not bad, not bad. You?'

'Not too bad, I guess. What have you gone for today?'

'The veggie club, with added bacon.'

'Ah, like what you've done there – the non-veggie veggie club.'

She gave a half-hearted laugh, and took another bite of her sandwich. It looked really rather tasty, but I tried not to get too distracted, and focused on the main task at hand – being nice (again).

'Really sorry about last night, Sarah – those drinks just dragged on a little longer than expected.'

'Don't be silly – I understand. You need your boy time.'

'What I'd really like, though, is a bit more Sarah time.'

Her facial expression warmed.

'Sarah time?'

'I know I've been a bit distant the last couple of weeks. I haven't been myself. I was just a bit conscious that you seem to be really busy all the time, so I didn't want you to think I was some kind of loser who hadn't anything to do with his time other than, you know, think about you.'

'Will! I'm so relieved. I really thought that you were just going off me.'

'Definitely not. Quite the opposite in fact.'

She put her sandwich down and reached across the table to grab my hand.

'Oh Will, you are a funny boy.'

'Funny strange or funny chuckle chuckle?'

'Both!'

We leant across the table for a bacon-roasted-pepper-avocado-mozzarella-and-light-mayonnaise-flavoured kiss. The sweetheart was back – although, I had to admit, I had the dickhead to thank.

Chapter 10

Going Exclusive:

Investment

I had managed to patch things up with Sarah. My bargaining power theory appeared to have worked. It seemed that my quest to find love using economic theory was heading in the right direction. Whether in the long run this meant I was heading for emotional stagnation, I still didn't know. I had made Sarah suffer a little by making myself less available, but at least it meant that she was now including me more in her life. Things seemed to be more equal, and it looked like we were on track for a full-blown relationship. I was happy. For now, at least.

But I still had my doubts. I just didn't know for sure whether I was ready to make that commitment. Being single was great, some of the time, but also, to be honest, pretty shit. I met with Flora to talk things over. She didn't mince her words, as usual.

'So when are you going to man up and ask Sarah out?' asked Flora.

'What do you mean, "ask her out"? I've already been seeing her for six weeks.'

'I know, but, have you *really* asked her out – have you had *the chat*?'

'What? Like the "so are we official" chat?'

'Exactly. She's a nice girl, Will. You've got to nail her down – girls like to know where they stand. She's probably going to think you're seeing other girls unless you show you're serious about her.'

'Flora, I'm not fifteen. I don't have to ask her "Will you be my girlfriend?" Can I not just, you know, see how things go? I'm sure we'll end up calling each other boyfriend and girlfriend eventually, I just don't think we need to label ourselves for the sake of it.'

'So, what you're really saying is you'll carry on seeing her until a better offer comes along.'

'No! Not at all. I like her. A lot.'

'Well, that's what she'll think unless you use the "g" word.'

'Bloody hell you girls are so insecure sometimes!'

'Will, you're the one who sends me text requests for girl advice at two in the morning – you're not exactly an emotional stronghold.'

'Point taken. What do you think I should do?'

'Will, you know what I think. She's a great girl. You should go for it, ask her out – there aren't many other girls like her at uni, you'd be an idiot not to.'

I clearly had some thinking to do. Was it the right time to say goodbye to being single? I wouldn't just be beginning a relationship, I would also be giving up a way of life. No more first dates. No more chatting up girls in nightclubs (or at least trying to). No more tales of heroic conquests to tell the boys. But it wouldn't be all bad.

There would be no more lonely nights in front of the TV, no more agonising over whether a girl liked me, and no more trudging home alone after a failed night out on the pull.

Being single, in short, had its highs and lows. It was great when it went well, but more than dreadful when it went badly. Being in a relationship, on the other hand, promised stability. Although I would miss out on the best bits of being single – the freedom and independence – in return I wouldn't have to put up with the worst bits – loneliness and rejection.

A clear trade-off had emerged. Before me I had the choice of either an exciting, yet volatile life as a single guy, or the more settled, secure life of a boyfriend. It was just like, it would appear, the choice faced by investors when deciding whether to put their money into risky stocks and shares or in the bank. By putting their money into stocks and shares investors can either make millions or lose everything overnight. If they put their money into a savings account, however, while they may be guaranteed a fixed rate of return (i.e. interest), they would be missing out in a big way if the market boomed and the stock prices went through the roof. Being single is like playing the stock market. Sometimes you strike lucky, and at other times you crash and burn. Being in a relationship, on the other hand, is more like putting money in the bank, as the feeling of knowing that your money is safe and growing, slowly, is similar to the feeling of the constant sense of happiness and security when you have someone in your life.

Rob, an economist friend of mine, sat me down and

gave me his view of the situation: the best choice for me depended on three things: 1) the market conditions – were there lots of good single girls out there, and how did Sarah compare?; 2) the *liquidity* of the assets available – did I want to be tied up with Sarah, or did I prefer to have the freedom to start seeing someone else when I felt like it?; 3) my appetite for risk – was I happy to put up with the lows to get the highs, or would I rather have smooth returns? He laid it out like a three-card trick and then stared at me like a Las Vegas dealer seeing which way I would jump.

So I worked through his three factors. First, **Market conditions.**

As Flora had mentioned, these weren't great. Being well into our first year at uni, the supply of good girls was drying up. It didn't look like I could become a millionaire overnight by playing the market. Sarah, in comparison, seemed like a good bet. Although things had been slightly tense between us as we had both tried to manoeuvre for control of the relationship, we had learnt to relax a little more now, and were getting to really know each other. As you've probably gathered, ever since Lizzie dumped me I had been feeling quite vulnerable. My confidence with girls was down, and Sarah seemed like a much-needed safe-haven from that world of uncertainty and dejection.

Going out with Sarah, as much as I hate to admit it, appeared to be a classic case of an investor, his nerves having been rattled by a volatile stock market, looking for peace of mind and investing in savings bonds where his money would be safe and his return guaranteed.

You are probably wondering why I wasn't worried about the prospect of going out with Sarah, given the lesson I'd learnt in Chapter 4 that if a girl appeared to be too good to be true then she probably was. The thing is, meeting Sarah made me realise that even if the market for relationships was perfectly informed, just because everyone had equal access to the information about the assets being traded, that didn't necessarily mean that they would all interpret the information in exactly the same way. Two perfectly rational investors may form completely different opinions, both of them credible in their own right, of the potential returns on an asset based on the same information. It may be that they have had experience with particular types of assets that makes them look at information available in a different way, or they may have been able to uncover hidden truths within the data that others don't see. That means that, however well-informed and skilful investors are, the market price of an asset is not always a completely reliable benchmark of value. In fact, the whole point of being an investor is to try and find assets with prices that *are* unreliable, insofar as their market price understates their real value. That's how people make money, and that was how I was going to get myself a great girlfriend.

Sarah, I thought, was one such undervalued asset. She was single, which suggested that the market didn't have strong demand for her, but from what I had seen, she had very strong fundamentals. Perhaps I had just misread her, or perhaps others just didn't see the same qualities in her that I did. I admit that viewing Sarah with the same level of excitement as investing in savings bonds sounds pretty harsh, but for all I knew, she'd be paying out bumper rates of interest for years to come.

Buy.

Next, **Liquidity.**

Of course, it isn't quite as simple as just looking at which girl I would be happiest with at any particular moment in time. When looking at investment choices, an investor can't only look at returns in comparison to what else is on offer. They also have to know how long they are going to be committed to that investment, and how quickly they can get out if it turns sour, or if something else better comes along.

As the name suggests, the *liquidity* of an asset refers to exactly this; how readily can you flow from one investment to the next? Or, more precisely, how quickly can you convert that asset into readily expendable cash? Stocks tend to be extremely liquid. You can buy and sell them practically in an instant, meaning that when an investor has got everything possible out of it, he can sell that stock and buy something else that he thinks will give him a better return. Savings bonds, on the other hand, are quite the opposite. They often require an investor to tie up his cash for several years. Although an investor might like the return he is getting on the bond initially, say 5 percent in comparison to a stock market which is only growing by an average of 3 percent, if there is a boom in the market and suddenly other investors are getting an average return of 6 percent, the savings bond investor can't do anything about it – he's committed to the full term of the bond.

Because his investment is *illiquid*, he'll just have to bite his lip while he sees other investment opportunities being snapped up around him.

Having illiquid assets, however, isn't always a bad thing. You might be losing some flexibility, but banks like to reward investors for tying up their cash for longer periods, as they too like certainty, only for different, but related, reasons: while I like the certainty of the guaranteed interest rate, the bank likes the certainty that the cash that people have invested won't be going anywhere for a fixed period of time. This allows banks to plan how to allocate resources effectively in the long term while not having to worry about investors pulling out their cash at any moment. In order to attract these longer-term investments, banks offer bigger rates of interest the longer you invest in the bond.

The same goes for relationships. The more you commit to one another, the more you are likely to get out of the relationship; loyalty does not go unrewarded. To take one example: the classic holiday booking dilemma. As everyone knows, booking in advance usually means cheaper holidays. So when a girl brings up summer holiday plans, probably at some point in the depths of winter, this appears, on the face of it, to be nothing more than a straightforward case of being organised and grabbing the bargain seats on easyJet while they last. Far from it. This can be a pivotal moment in a young relationship. Booking a summer holiday in winter is committing yourself to the relationship for at least the period before and during the holiday. Buying one £50 air fare can therefore drastically reduce the liquidity of your investment.

For those who are having doubts about whether they want to stay in the relationship, this can be an exceptionally awkward conversation:

> *'Honey, shall we go on holiday together next summer? I know it's only November, but there are some really good deals at the moment.'*
>
> *'Yeah, sure, sounds like a great idea. Let's have a really good think about where we want to go.'*
>
> *'I was thinking Greece. It's always fantastic weather and there's great night life – how about it?'*
>
> *'Mmm. Greece. I'm not sure about that.'*
>
> *'Why?'*
>
> *'Er, it's just that I've never really been a hummus fan – can't stand the stuff. And don't even get me started on taramasalata. '*
>
> *'Er, OK. Well let's think of somewhere else we'd both like to go.'*
>
> *'Yes, let's. We've got ages to think about it, so let's not make any rushed decisions.'*

Of course, whenever either the girl or the boy is this anxious about committing themselves to being together at some point far in the future, and they choose just to take each day as it comes, while they may benefit from keeping their options open, they inevitably miss out on some potentially bigger returns. I'm not only talking about cheap holiday deals, but also about the feeling that you are building towards a future together. I was yet to ever really experience anything like this, but I wanted to see if I could get there with Sarah. Otherwise, frankly, what would be the point of a relationship at all?

Buy.

And finally, **risk-appetite.**

It was looking like Sarah got a big tick in the first two boxes. She seemed as if she was a strong, safe investment relative to the rest of the market, and I was confident that sacrificing the freedom, the liquidity, of being single to be with her would be worth it. But there was one final factor to weigh up; was my risk appetite suited to being in a relationship? Or would I miss the occasional thrill of being single? There certainly have been times in my life where I have relished uncertainty, and other times when I have been more risk-averse. I cast my mind back to one of the most enjoyable periods of my life: driving across America on my gap year with an old school friend, Jonny. We were in the mood for taking risks.

We had just arrived in post-Katrina New Orleans on the Fourth of July 2006, and the party was already getting started. We'd been staying in hostels and cheap motels for the whole trip so far, but this time we hesitated. The music was already pumping out of the bars – we didn't have any time to lose looking for a place to stay. We tried to think of quick solutions, but there only appeared to be one: we were going to play 'sex or freeze'.

We'd heard about this game from a guy we'd met in a hostel in New York. The concept was pretty simple. You turn up in a city with nowhere to stay, but rather than forking out for a room, you just risk it: either you pull that night and go back to hers ('sex'), or you spend the night out on the streets ('freeze'). When we were first told about this game we were pretty appalled. We dismissed it as an act of desperation, not something that you'd choose to do for fun. We were only innocent(ish) 19-year-olds after all. But the balmy French Quarter, which was sprawling with daiquiri-sipping girls in stars and stripes bikinis, was already soaked with sexual tension, and it clearly went to our heads. We were going to go for it.

By eight in the evening the official parades were over, and the streets quickly gave way to a steady flow of patriots-turned-sweat-soaked-party-goers. Jonny and I had also got stuck into the daiquiris, using our fake IDs that we'd had made before coming over to the States. After several weeks of travelling from city to city, we had perfected the art of how to exploit our main asset when it came to attracting American girls: our accents. I say 'art', but that may be a little generous. Essentially all it involved was talking to each other, loudly and ostentatiously, within eavesdropping range of a group of girls:

ME: Jonathan, what do you say to us getting several pints of lager beer here before heading to a local diner for a hamburger and chips, with, needless to say, a generous helping of tomato ketchup?

JONNY: William, I must say I agree with you there – excellent suggestion, if I may say so.

Girl overhears us.

AMERICAN GIRL: Hey, I'm sorry for interrupting, but are you guys, are you guys *British*?

JONNY: (*looking surprised*) Yes we are as it so happens, how could you tell?

AMERICAN GIRL: Oh-my-God! Your accents are so cute! Girls, come over here a-sap, these guys are *British*.

The next half an hour would be taken up with the usual pronunciation comparison game (*parsta v pasta, baathroom v barthroom, toob v tewb* etc.). By then, hopefully, Jonny and I would be well on our way to a snog. Tonight, however, we needed accommodation for the night, so we were probably going to need a lot more than well accentuated Rs and vowels.

By 1am, I was convinced that my gamble had paid off. I had bumped into a girl, Lauren, on the dance floor of a western-themed nightclub (bucking bronco, swinging doors, and bargirls in cowboy hats all included), and hit it off straight away, no pronunciation game required. Jonny, on the other hand, had befriended a bunch of college students who had rented a nearby apartment for the weekend, and was told he was welcome to sleep on their sofa. He may not have been on for the 'sex' part of the game, but at least he was guaranteed a roof over his head. Mine was by no means a guarantee, but I was sure that another hour or so of hard work would secure me a place to stay.

The crunch moment came when Jonny and his bunch called it a night around two in the morning. Lauren had hinted that I could come back to hers, but I could tell that her friend, who had dragged her away on a couple of occasions to give her a stern talking to, wasn't so keen on the idea. Nonetheless, when Jonny offered me the chance to join them, I still felt pretty bullish, and decided to back myself – 'this one is in the bag' I told him. As I saw him head down the street, I realised I had just effectively put everything on red.

Soon after Jonny left, Lauren told me to stay put on the dance floor while she went to the bar to grab us a glass of water (and God did we need it – the place was steaming like a sauna, and both of our backs were soaked through).[25] I hung around for a few minutes, gingerly shuffling my feet around to the music, trying to keep her in view – I couldn't afford to lose her. But then, like an eagle saving its offspring from danger, her friend took her chance to swoop and had her out of the door in an instant. I fought my way through the dance floor to try and salvage the situation, but by the time I got out onto the street she was nowhere to be seen.

The enormity of my situation then hit me. I was alone in New Orleans with nowhere to stay, and, rather conveniently, my pay-as-you-go phone was out of credit so I had no means of contacting Jonny. Jonny had also kept hold of the car keys, so I didn't even have the option of spending the night in the car. The game was lost – my chips had been raked in and the banker had shut up shop for the night.

I tried desperately to find someone to take me in for the night. I approached complete strangers, hoping that my English accent would instil sufficient trust for them not to take me for any other drunken student. But, sympathetic though they were, no one had a bed or sofa to offer

---

25 Gross, but a pretty standard feature of a night out in New Orleans, apparently.

me. The streets were now practically deserted, and the street cleaners were out in force blasting away the night's excesses with high-pressured hoses.

After 15 minutes of searching, I saw a police patrol car parked on one of the side streets. There was only one option left – I was going to have to turn myself in as an underage drinker, and spend a night in a cell. I knocked on the police car's window, which the officer duly lowered.

'Is there a problem?'

'Officer, I'm terribly sorry to bother you, but I've got a confession to make – I'm only nineteen years old and I've been drinking, heavily, all night. I think you should arrest me.' He looked unimpressed.

'Do you have some place to go, kid?'

'No, that's kind of the problem.'

'You're looking for a place to stay,? What do you think we are – some kind of motel service?'

'What, you're not going to arrest me?'

'Good night, kid,' the officer said as he wound up his window.

Now I really was screwed. Clearly the New Orleans police had bigger things to worry about than locking up underage drinkers on Independence Day. I sat in a nearby porch, holding my head in my hands, my mouth so dry that I was unable to swallow. The streets were now completely deserted. I looked at my watch – 3.30am. That meant I only had to stay awake for about another three hours until it got light again, and maybe about five until Jonny woke up and got in touch to see if things had gone to plan. As long as I stayed in the French Quarter, the most touristy bit of New Orleans and the least affected by the hurricane damage from the year before, I convinced myself I would be OK. Then my phone rang. Never had the Nokia melody sounded so sweet; it was Jonny.

'Will, how are you? Are you with Lauren?'

'Jonny, I can't tell you how pleased I am to hear your voice.'

'Why? What's happened?'

'Let's just say that things didn't work out. Where are you?'

'Ha, I knew you were being too cocky with that girl! Her friend saw what you were up to a mile off – you didn't have a chance!'

I could always trust Jonny to see the bigger picture on a night when sleeping in a police cell seemed, for a time, to be my best chance of making it through the night alive.

'Jonny, now really isn't the time – I just need to get some sleep.'

Jonny directed me to the apartment where he was staying which was only a couple of blocks away. He took me into the living room which was full wall-to-wall with passed out students, and showed me the part of the floor that I had been allocated. I squeezed myself in to the gap, my face sandwiched between some guy's backside and some girl's feet. To this day, I don't think I've ever lain on a more comfortable floor than on that night in New Orleans.

Clearly, taking risks like the one Jonny and I took on Independence Day 2006 doesn't always pay off. But it's not always about actually getting that end pay-off. The feeling of taking the risk is, in itself, regardless of the outcome, a sort of pay-off. It's exciting, it makes you feel alive. Having no idea how your night is going to end can fill the more risk-averse types with dread and anxiety – they would much rather know for certain where they're sleeping, even if it means that they miss out on any potential upsides of leaving it to chance. For others, the risk-loving types, the very fact that taking risks involves uncertainty, and therefore a much wider range of possible outcomes, some good, some bad, is what makes them attracted to taking risky courses of action. They just accept that to get it good, you will sometimes have to get it really, really bad.

Although I looked back fondly on the days when I relished uncertainty, things were different now. I simply wasn't getting the return I needed in order to justify the risks associated with being a single guy, and I now yearned for the security, the certainty, of a steady relationship. There was only one thing I could rationally do: I was going to ask Sarah out, officially.

Our relationship became official at approximately 2.30am on the night of the Economics Society Ball. Sarah had, respectfully, declined my offer of a plus one – 'you go and enjoy yourself with your classmates' she said, clearly trying, and failing, to conceal her horror at the prospect of making conversation with a group of socially awkward boys whose idea of a fun night in was making rude shapes on their graphing calculators (apparently just talking to me was already enough of a challenge, she jested). After a two-course dinner of fish mousse (of unspecified variety) and desiccated chicken breast with liquidised mashed potato,[26] a fairly routine series of drinking games, and the

---

26 It goes without saying that the Economics Society would only tolerate the finest cuisine available.

ordeal of the 95 percent male disco,[27] I decided to call it a night. On the off-chance that Sarah was still awake, I gave her a call, not really thinking that she might be remotely pissed-off with me for calling so late, or non-receptive to the idea of having me over to stay. To my delight, she answered.

'Will?'

'Sarah, hey, are you still up?'

'No, I've been sleeping – what time is it?'

'Time for me to come over?'

'No, really, what time is it?'

'It's just gone two.'

'Bloody hell, Will, it's late.'

'I know, I know, I just wanted to see you.'

'OK, but just so you know, there's no way I'm having sex with you.'

'Understood.' (Still worth a try though, I thought.)

I hopped on a night-bus to Sarah's. She opened the door in her full length pyjama bottoms and baggy t-shirt, and pressed her finger to her lips to tell me to keep my voice down. I exaggeratedly tip-toed into her flat, and, as anyone would having been greeted by a girl like Sarah, nuzzled my mouth against her neck. She seemed to enjoy it, but then gently pushed me away.

'OK, Will, not now, bedtime,' Sarah said, as if she was telling an overexcited dog to go to its basket.

I obediently followed her through to her room and into bed. As soon as I got in, to my disappointment, she rolled over away from me and scrunched the duvet into

---

27 This usually involved encircling the handful of girls that were brave enough to turn up, and plenty of air guitar, of course.

her chest, a clear anti-snuggle measure.

'How was your night, Sarah?' I asked, hopefully.

'Fine, you?' she replied, remarkably, muffled by her pillow.

'Quite fun actually. Would have been nicer if you were there though,' I said, softly stroking her back.

'Good, now can we go to sleep?'

'Can I just ask you one quick question though, Sarah?'

'Mmm?'

'I was just thinking, we've been seeing each other for a few weeks now, and I'd really like it if you would be, you know, be *my girl.*'

Sarah unscrunched her duvet and rolled over to face me.

'Do you mean be, like, your *girlfriend*?'

'Yeah, that's kind of what I meant.'

'Awww, Will, that's so sweet of you to ask! I don't think anyone's asked me that since I was 15! [*I told you so, Flora.*] Of course I'll be your girlfriend.'

She rolled over on top of me and gave me a big kiss on the lips. My investment offer had been accepted, and if the butterflies in my stomach were anything to go by, this one was for the long term. The Romantic Economist had succeeded.

Chapter 11

Fruit Punch and Flirtatious Girlfriends:
The Strategy of Conflict

I had officially been going out with Sarah for three weeks. Things were great, really great. Those butterflies had fully colonised my stomach, and she had gone down a treat with the parents. Now it was the even more important test: introducing her to my closest friends. I hate to say it, but having the approval of my friends was essential to the success of the relationship. I like to think that I am independent-minded and confident in my own taste, but a single remark that suggested that I wasn't quite on to the winner I thought I was tended to make me feel totally deluded. Suddenly my love interest would change from a beautiful, funny girl with striking facial features and a good sense of humour to a girl with a big nose, bushy eyebrows and an annoying laugh. A nod of approval or pat on the back, on the other hand, make me think that I was the luckiest guy on the planet.

The crucial introduction was going to be at Max's birthday party. All my friends were going, and so it was an ideal opportunity to introduce, and show off, Sarah to them.

Sarah was a really lovely-looking girl, and like many guys in my situation, I couldn't help but feel a sense of pride in introducing her to my friends. I strode into the flat, Sarah in tow, with the swagger of a caveman who has just returned to his tribe having single-handedly slain a mammoth: 'Look what I have captured! Me, big, strong, powerful man!'

I bumped into a couple of familiar faces.

'Kate, I'd like you to meet my *girlfriend*, Sarah.'

I couldn't have made the fact that she was my girl-friend, my catch, and my prize, any more obvious. People don't go for the 'g' word so early on unless they're rather pleased with themselves. Kate then did a customary head-to-toe scan, the human equivalent of a bottom sniff, subtly concealed behind a compliment about the dress Sarah was wearing. She liked what she saw; while Sarah was tempo-rarily distracted by the flat-party punch (a combination of Tesco Value Vodka and rum, with a splash of Five Alive), Kate gave me a quick thumbs-up. Thank God. She'd been approved.

Now I had the vote of confidence from a female friend, it was time for the next, undoubtedly harsher, judges: the men.

I introduced Sarah to a couple of friends of mine, Rob and Tom. Rob was one of those guys who, for whatever reason, girls find completely irresistible. Sure, he was good-looking, but he was no Adonis. He just had charm, and a killer instinct. In spite of Rob's prolific record, I felt confident enough to leave him and Tom with Sarah so they could get to know her properly without my adoration for her obscuring their first impressions.

Now this may seem a little objectionable, but there is an unwritten rule amongst mates that if it is somehow adjudged that a friend's new girlfriend is in fact far too good for them she remains fair game to hit on.[28] I was aware I was risking this, particularly with Rob, but Sarah and I were going strong, and so leaving her unattended for a few minutes didn't really bother me – not at first anyway.

After a few minutes of being apart from Sarah I noticed from the far side of the room that not only were Rob and Tom flirting with her, which was to be expected, but also that she was flirting with them, quite heavily. They appeared to be laughing rather a lot. I'd never seen Sarah laugh that much before. She was so animated, giggling away at practically everything they said. She touched Rob on the shoulder, leaning into him, as if to say that she couldn't take it anymore. Then I felt something in my gut more intensely than ever before: jealousy, that lethal concoction of adrenaline with a sense of impending loss that can drive men to madness. I tried to ignore it.

'Stay cool, Will, you've got nothing to worry about,' I thought to myself, as I sucked the last dregs from the bottom of a can of beer. I stared straight through the girl I was talking to as I tried to work out my next move. I couldn't just let this happen. I had to show Sarah, and everyone else in the room, that I was in control. But I didn't want to come across as an overprotective, untrusting

---

28 Any behaviour that has to be described as 'fair game' to justify it, however, almost certainly isn't.

boyfriend, who steps into any conversation as soon as hands start wandering and seductive glances become more than merely fleeting. One of the things that had attracted me to Sarah in the first place was her bubbliness. To intervene now would not only reveal my insecurity, but also stop her from being herself.

I let their conversation continue a little longer. Tom had now left Rob to do his stuff on his own, and the flirting had gone up a couple of notches as a result. Their smatterings of laughter became louder to the point where it was just about all I could hear in the room. Each time their bodies touched, I could feel a sharp electric prod in my side. I felt sick, the jealousy spreading to every part of my body. The girl I was talking to could tell that something wasn't right. She asked me if everything was OK, and when I told her no, the reason being that I was convinced my girlfriend was about to run off to the nearest bedroom with Rob – he was accustomed to doing this at parties (although not normally with his friend's girlfriends) – the girl said that I had to step in immediately and take control. She was right: I had to act.

I walked over to Sarah and Rob with a drink in each hand. I handed one to Sarah.

'How are you two getting on?' I asked, trying to come across as though I had been completely oblivious to the scenes of treachery I had seen unfolding from the other side of the room.

'Very well thanks, Will. Sarah is quite a catch, how did someone like you end up with a beautiful girl like this?' Rob said cheerily. The tone may have been complementary, but the essence was poison. I can't tell you how much I wanted to hit him right then.

Before I had time to come up with a suitably self-deprecating reply, Sarah put her arm around my back, stroking me gently. God that felt good. It was like sinking into a warm bath after a tough day, the stress that had built up inside me diffusing in an instant.

'You have such nice friends, Will,' Sarah said. 'Can you introduce me to some more?'

'Of course, let's have a wander. See you later, Rob,' I said, really thinking 'Fuck you, you cheating, handsome bastard.'

Few are strangers to that gut-wrenching situation I was in at that flat party. Do you go in early, exert your control, but risk coming across as insecure? Or do you do nothing until the last possible moment, or perhaps nothing at all, and come across as secure but lacking control? Again, as in Chapter 7, the answer to this seems to revolve around giving off the right signal. Insecure, jealous people are not willing to tolerate the emotional cost of their girlfriends flirting with others, and so will barely leave their side at a party. A secure guy, who knows that however much anyone hits on his girlfriend he will be the one taking her home, is willing to accept that cost. When the flirting becomes excessive, however, a timely intervention will still be required. Where can we find the right balance?

Imagine for a moment that we are endowed with a certain amount of emotional security. Some of us have lots of it, and can tolerate just about any degree of flirting by our girlfriend or boyfriend with others at parties. The flirting would be verging on full-on-snogging before they would be inclined to do anything about it. Others, on the other hand, have eggshell personalities, and try to wrap their girlfriends in cotton wool to stop any potential advances from morally wayward boys. Someone need only look their girlfriend in the eye (or anywhere else, for that matter) before they come swooping in to mark their territory.

Let's look at this financially. Let us imagine that our level of emotional security is the balance in our emotional security account. The more our girlfriend flirts with another guy, the more is drawn from that account. When the balance drops to a certain point at which we feel the need to exert our control, we intervene. We stop her eating away at the emotional funds we have entrusted her with. Generally speaking, the more control we have, the earlier we intervene in the situation. As you've probably already gathered, these two signals, security and control, can conflict. If we go in early, we are seen as someone who is in control of the relationship but has little emotional security. If we go in late, we can be seen as someone with lots of emotional security, but little control. Before this gets any more complicated, it's best that I show you exactly what I mean on a graph (Figure 7).

Here we have emotional security on the vertical axis and the time our girlfriend is flirting with another boy on the horizontal axis. People start with different amounts of emotional security: A, stonehearted; B, just about normal; and C, nervous wreck. The longer our girlfriend flirts, the more emotional security is drawn from our account, making the line slope downwards. The vertical lines represent how controlling we are — the more we like to keep our girlfriends under our thumb — the earlier we

FIGURE 7: Emotional security balance over time

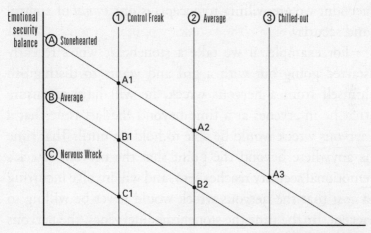

intervene; 1 is the control freak, whereas 3 is pretty chilled out. The points at which these lines cross are where each type of person intervenes. Say, for instance, we are moderately secure (B), and moderately controlling (2), then we intervene at point B2, which is just about the time when our girlfriend has started to touch the guy she is flirting with. If we are really insecure (C) and a control freak (1), on the other hand, we intervene at C1, the point at which the guy has just started talking to our girlfriend.

The problem is, although we may know what type of person we are, whether consciously or sub-consciously, our new girlfriends, and the people around us, don't. They can only tell what type of boyfriend we are by the timing of our intervention (here we are assuming, for simplicity, that the manner of the intervention in each case is identical, although of course in reality this would not be the case). How long we are willing to wait, and therefore how much of a cost to our emotional security account we are willing to accept, is our *signal* of control and security.

For example, if we take a stoneheart who's recently started going out with a girl and wants to distinguish himself from a nervous wreck, he will have to ensure that he intervenes at a time beyond the last time that a nervous wreck would be able to hold on until. That time is anywhere beyond the point that the nervous wreck's emotional security reaches zero, and will involve incurring a cost that the nervous wreck would never be willing to accept. By the time the stoneheart intervenes, the nervous wreck should be fast approaching their overdraft limit in their emotional security account.

Sometimes, however, we can get these signals wrong. The points at which the lines cross may be the optimal point for each type of person to intervene, but we can easily stray from that optimum by intervening earlier than we ideally should. If we are emotionally secure (A) and uncontrolling (3), but we decide to intervene at point A1, rather than wait until A3, we have inadvertently given off a signal that could be interpreted as one given off by an ultra-controlling nervous wreck (C1). This is because despite having plenty of emotional security left in our account, and being able to wait a lot longer, our poor timing has meant that the chilled-out stonehearts (A3s) cannot be distinguished from the control-freak nervous wrecks (C1s) as they have intervened at the time that would be optimal for a nervous wreck, rather than a stoneheart. They would meet a similar fate to the dick-heads and sweethearts in Chapter 7, who, by taking their dates out to a generic restaurant, both gave off the same *observationally equivalent* signal, despite being different types of person.

It would be useful for me to explain at this point why the subtitle to this chapter is 'The Strategy of Conflict'. Basically, I confess, the reason is that the thinking behind this chapter is lifted straight out of one of my favourite books on game theory and information economics – Thomas Schelling's *The Strategy of Conflict*. Schelling saw that signalling security and control are fundamental tools of statecraft, and he used US foreign policy in the Pacific, following the Second World War, as an example of how an early intervention to eliminate a potential threat can inadvertently signal weakness, rather than strength.

A small Chinese warship had strayed into US-occupied Japanese waters. Although the ship posed no real threat to the immense US military force that was present in Japan, their decision to sink the ship as a sign of strength and control over the area may have actually created exactly the opposite effect. A country with a tight grip on the area would have been willing to accept such a small intrusion. Not reacting at all would be like taunting the enemy with words such as 'it's going to take a lot more than your little warship to scare us, China.' A country that had shakier foundations, on the other hand, would sink the ship more as a knee-jerk reaction than as a considered, strategic move. Of course, if a country became willing to accept small intrusions into their waters on a regular basis without intervening, that too could signal a lack of control in the area. Much like the scene I was faced with at the flat party, the US therefore had to balance the two conflicting signals; go in strong, and risk coming across as weak, or go in late, or not at all, and risk being seen as lacking control over the situation.

In the end I went in somewhere between B2 and A3. Was that the right choice? My emotional security account took one hell of a beating, and was in desperate need of funds. But I had been quite cool, which plays well with girls. I was also left wondering if girls flirt as a means of testing their boyfriends. They are probably thinking, how well does he cope with the battlefield situation? What's his reaction when I put him in the position of the Americans in post-WWII Japan?

To pass this test, do girls want early intervention, which demonstrates commitment, or do they like late intervention, which is cool? Or, even more alarmingly, might they want both, the insatiable demand which establishes their own authority in the relationship?

B2/A3, on this evidence anyway, does get results. Sarah and I left the flat party hand in hand. It had gone well. My friends really liked her (Rob perhaps more than others). I was beginning to get excited about being with her for a long time. My mind was awash with romantic weekends away, fun days out in London, and, God help me, I was even wondering whether she might be 'the one.'

Chapter 12

Hiding the Crazy:
Credible Threats

It was really happening. I had smashed through the six-week barrier with Sarah, and she had not yet shown any signs of losing interest. For me, this was a particularly significant feat. In my previous relationships, the six-week mark had been marred by the agonising self-doubt that inevitably follows those dreamy first few weeks with someone new. This was usually the first point at which both parties adopt a slightly more pragmatic approach to the relationship: thoughts stray from 'aren't we having a lovely time' to 'is this really going to go anywhere?' For the first time, the answer to this question was a resounding yes.

Things had moved beyond the game-playing days, and I was now finally able to relish having a constant female presence in my life. Her soft skin, her yummy scent, her pretty clothes, her sweet, gentle voice. After years of living in an all-boys school, and then with three other boys at university, these were all things that I had only ever really experienced momentarily. Now they were all forming a regular feature of my daily routine, all embodied in the wonderful, angelic Sarah. Wow, girls are amazing, I thought.

What made Sarah particularly wonderful was her apparently never-ending tolerance of all the annoying (and, I admit, disgusting) little habits that I had picked up from my time in an all-male environment: leaving used teabags by kettles, beds unmade, sheets and towels unwashed for weeks at a time, and, of course, watching TV with my hands down my trousers. She barely even flinched when she saw the state of my room when she first came to stay. Instead, she just skipped over weeks' worth of dirty laundry and jumped on the bed, not passing a single word of judgment.

I genuinely thought that this capacity for forgiveness might be limitless the Saturday morning I farted in bed. It was so smelly it woke both of us up. I was completely mortified. For a moment I thought she was either going to be sick, or throw herself out of the window in an effort to escape the toxic fumes, and then have me referred to a doctor before quietly forgetting that I had ever existed. But she didn't. She just gave off a half-hearted protest, 'Oh William, what did you eat last night?' before rolling over and giving me a good morning snuggle. But the smell was still really bad, so we thought it best to get up and have breakfast.

It wasn't only in domestic situations that she showed this remarkable ability to cast aside my typically male undesirables. She was also able to contain any signs of frustration whenever I was at all annoyingly vague in my social plans.

'So, Will, what are you doing this weekend?'

'Not really sure. Probably just going to watch the rugby and have a few beers.'

'Oh, OK, well just let me know if you want to do anything.'

You would expect most girlfriends in such a situation to tell me to sort my life out, and make the most of the weekend by arranging to do something nice together. But not Sarah. She was happy for us to leave plans to the last minute. She understood guys like me. She liked me for the complete package, for all my various imperfections as well as my good parts. I really couldn't believe my luck. Some of my friends' girlfriends would have been all over them for the type of behaviour I was getting away with. Clearly I had landed the perfect girlfriend. Or so I thought.

A few more weeks passed, and we were beginning to settle into the routine of a typical university relationship. We started to spend nights in together, have practically every meal together, and walk to lectures together. I was in heaven. My only regret was that it had taken me this long to get a girlfriend this great. It made my life better in practically all areas. The tone of the relationship, however, took a sharp turn on the day I handed in a particularly gruesome piece of coursework, and I was out having some beers with my economics friends.

Sarah and I had spent a few nights apart while I put in some late evenings at the library to get the coursework finished. For three nights on the trot I had been holed up in the 'bunker', the infamous underground 24-hour access computer lab, where students would miraculously pull off 4000-word essays in a night, fuelled entirely by a combination of adrenaline and the 50p instant coffee from the Klix vending machine.[29]

We had arranged to have dinner at Sarah's to celebrate hand-in day. This was the longest that we had been apart since we first started seeing each other, and I really couldn't wait to see her. What I hadn't appreciated, however, was the extent to which the only thing keeping me awake was the pressure of a looming deadline. With the deadline now met, and a couple of beers already swiftly put away, the adrenaline in my system had been completely washed out, and it wasn't long before I was propping myself up against the bar, fighting to keep my eyes open, and clenching my jaw each time a yawn tried to surface.

'Will, you haven't said anything in 20 minutes, are you OK?' asked one of my classmates.

'I'm sorry, guys, I'm completely whacked. I haven't had much sleep these past few days.'

'Oh boo hoo, Will, does someone need a little kip?'

Not realising they were taking the piss, I nodded my head, and rolled out my lower lip as if I was a child wanting to be taken to bed by his parents.

'Awww, isn't that sweet. Taxi for one then!'

I was too tired to feel embarrassed. I just left the rest of my pint on the bar, said goodbye, and headed for home. I couldn't face the tube journey to Sarah's, I just needed my bed. I knew she would understand, and I called her up to make my excuses.

'Sarah, hi, it's Will.'

'Will! Hi! Are you coming on over then, I'm just about

---

29 Some even resorted to the yellow powdered soup of unspecified flavour to keep them going.

to put the shepherd's pie in the oven.'

Oh God, I thought, she's cooked me shepherd's pie. She must have remembered that was the first thing I had learnt how to cook. That made what I was about to tell her even harder.

'Sarah, I'm so sorry but I don't think I'm going to be able to make it over tonight. I'm completely shattered. I won't be much fun. I just need to go to bed.'

I expected a lovely, sweet, understanding voice to make me feel less bad for flaking on her. Her response came as a big shock.

'Oh thanks, Will, that's just great. So I've cooked this shepherd's pie, your favourite, for nothing. You should have just told me that you would be too tired to come over tonight rather than mess me around.'

I thought for a second that I should tell her, to provide some kind of consolation, that shepherd's pie wasn't actually my favourite, it was just the first thing I had learnt how to cook, but somehow I felt that might not help. I realised that I was dealing with a completely new situation. She wasn't her usual sweet, patient and forgiving self; she was actually angry with me.

'Sarah, I'm so sorry, I thought you'd understand. You know how hard I have been working recently. I just had a couple of beers with my classmates and it just hit me. I didn't know I would be this tired.'

'So you're fine to have a couple of beers with your friends but you're too tired to come and see me. Well it's good to know where I stand, at least. You're not the only one who has been working hard this week, you know.'

It was like I was speaking to a different person. I admit

I was being a bit of a shit, but I had been a bit of a shit in the past and I hadn't been subjected to this kind of outburst before. I didn't know how to take it.

'Sarah, Sarah, Sarah, please don't be like this. I'll make it up to you, I promise.'

'Well it's a bit late now.'

Sensing the possibility of lasting damage, I caved in.

'OK, Sarah, I'm on my way. I'm getting on the tube now, I'll be at yours in half an hour max.'

'Don't trouble yourself if you're too "tired" to see me, Will.'

'No, honestly it's fine. I don't know what got into me. I'll see you soon.'

'OK, fine. Hurry up.'

I sheepishly made my way over to Sarah's, knowing that I would have some serious ground to make up. I was buzzed up to her flat, and was greeted by the delicious homely smell of freshly cooked shepherd's pie wafting down the stairwell. I knocked on the door, not knowing whether to expect a big hug and kiss or an angry tirade. I was, for the first time since our early dating days, a little nervous (or perhaps even scared) to see her.

She opened the door, and slowly emerged from the din of the hallway. There was just about enough light for me to see that she had been crying. She didn't say anything.

'Oh Sarah, I'm so sorry.'

I went in for the hug, and tried to kiss her on the cheek, but she pulled away.

'I really can't believe you sometimes, Will.'

'Sometimes? What do you mean? This is the first time anything like this has happened. It's the first time I have seen you so upset with me.'

'Will, this isn't the first time you've ditched me for your friends. And these weren't even your real friends – they were your economics friends. How do you think that made me feel?'

'Oh come on, Sarah, my economics friends aren't that bad! They're actually quite normal, once you get to know them.'

'Will! I'm being serious. I think it's about time you started taking this relationship a bit more seriously.'

'I do take it seriously. I'm completely crazy about you.'

'Well, a few things have to change then.'

'Like what?'

'Let's not talk about it now, the pie is getting cold.'

She gave me the kiss that I had been yearning for all week, and we sat down to enjoy her delicious shepherd's pie. She had even remembered to put in my secret ingredient, mango chutney, which gave the meat a sweet, comforting flavour, and had smoothed the mashed potato with a fork to make it look like a ploughed field, just the way I like it. By the time we headed to bed, I felt as if all had been forgotten and normality had been resumed. I fell to sleep as soon as my head hit the pillow, now reassured by the fact that we had survived our first major argument.

But from that night onwards something changed. The relationship as a whole was going strong, but her tolerance of my misdemeanours, bit by bit, cock-up by cock-up, seemed to diminish. Soon I found that none of my various shortcomings, which I had previously mistakenly believed to form a part of what Sarah found appealing about me, in an 'ah, isn't he so adorability incompetent/ unhygienic' kind of way, were going unnoticed:

'Will! I told you not to leave the loo seat up!'

'Will! When was the last time you washed your sheets?' and

'Will! This is the third time this week you've been late!'

Of course, I was far too crazy about Sarah by this stage to find any of these nagging commands a reason to start going off her. She could do no wrong. Anyhow, it wasn't as if she was being particularly unreasonable. These were all things that I needed to sort out: leaving the loo seat up is inconsiderate, clean sheets are much nicer to sleep in, and being late is just plain rude. Soon she had me dancing to her tune, and I didn't really have a problem with it. Naturally, though, this didn't go unnoticed amongst the boys, who liked nothing better than to accuse a friend of being 'pussy-whipped'.

'Looks like Sarah's got you on a pretty tight leash!' said Freddie, as he came into my room when I was giving it its first hoovering since we had moved in, almost six months before. 'I've never seen your room looking this tidy as long as I've known you!'

He was right. All my clothes were now either neatly folded away in their designated drawer, or in my brand-new Ikea linen basket, and my books and files were all neatly lined up and labelled on the bookshelf, rather than sprawled on the floor and desk as usual.

'Well, you know, it was about time I gave this room a good sort out. I've been meaning to do it for ages.'

'You mean since Sarah stopped hiding the crazy.'

'Hiding the crazy?'

'Oh come on, Will, you must know what I'm talking about. Girls are always much nicer to us in the first couple of months. They let you get away with murder. If they like you, you could probably wear the same boxers for five days straight and they wouldn't say anything. They don't want you to think that they're complete psychos, so they act all nice and forgiving. Once they're sure you've fallen for them, that's when they start turning the screw.'

'You mean Sarah has been acting nice all this time?'

'Will, there's a reason that none of us hang out in your room. It stinks. So either Sarah doesn't have a sense of smell, or she's been hiding the crazy, and she's just unleashed it on you.'

I tried to absorb the implications of this fresh insight into female relationship strategy. It was ingenious.

'You've got to give it to her, that's kind of clever.'

'Sure is, it gets us every time.'

I finished off my hoovering, and lay on my freshly made bed, my head nicely cushioned by the extra pillows that Sarah had brought round for me (she had told me that a bed doesn't look quite right unless you have at least two square coloured pillows resting on top, so gave me a couple of her spares). I thought about what Freddie had told me. It was all beginning to make sense.

Sarah's recent change in behaviour was all part of a grand strategy. It's always been apparent to me, mainly by observing my friends' girlfriends rather than through personal experience, that girls love the idea that they can change a man, and mend his wayward habits. Forgive me if this sounds a little cynical, but it's a bit like a pet project.

They start with a nice boy who is a little bit rough around the edges, and put him through their own personalised finishing school, all with the aim of creating their own model boyfriend who is good mannered, well turned out, and pleasant to live with. Ideally, girls, I imagine, would like to get to work straight away (and who wouldn't – boys can be kind of gross), but the only problem is that guys don't really like being nagged, and especially not from day one.

The girls' answer, as so brilliantly executed by my wonderful Sarah, is to just suck it up for the first few months, and only start kicking up a fuss once they know that their boyfriends simply love them too much to mind, or even notice, that they're being nagged. If Sarah had said something along the lines of 'bloody hell, Will, it stinks in here, you've got to sort out your room!' the first time she came over, although I would have probably taken the criticism on board (it did stink), I don't think I would have been too keen on the idea of having a head-mistress for a girlfriend, and my attraction towards her would have quickly cooled. Instead she started nudging me toward the proper, civilised way of doing things bit by bit, knowing that the longer we were together, the more she could afford to be more severe in her criticism of my habits. As with any other relationship between variables, this is best shown using a graph (Figure 8).

The graph shows two variables over time: the girl's propensity to forgive a boy's shortcomings, and the boy's level of emotional attachment to the girl. As you can see, at the start of the relationship the girl starts off at their most forgiving (the point at which she is said to be 'hiding

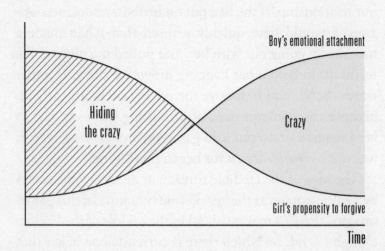

FIGURE 8: Hiding the crazy, and then showing it

Boy's emotional attachment

Hiding
the crazy

Crazy

Girl's propensity to forgive

Time

the crazy'), and the boy's level of emotional attachment is at its lowest. But over time, as the boy becomes more emotionally attached to the girl, the girl can start to pick up more and more on the boy's misdemeanours, up to the point where the boy is so deeply and madly in love with the girl and that she can afford to let no slip-up go unpunished.

Another variable that could be included on this graph is the boy's improvement in behaviour over time. Taking me as an example, as my emotional attachment to Sarah was growing, and therefore her propensity to punish or criticise me was increasing, it was in my interests to sharpen up my act (hence the hoovering and multiple pillows), otherwise I was at risk of losing her. At the beginning of the relationship, on the other hand, I could get away with my old habits because I had not yet developed the level of emotional attachment that Sarah needed to instigate her disciplinary regime without prejudicing our relationship. If she had put on her bossy boots straight away, I would have quickly realised that I had made a mistake by going out with her, and pulled the plug on the relationship before her nagging drove me crazy. In other words, Sarah had to forgive me for my cock-ups early on because the consequences of punishing me were not in her interests, or, to put it in game-theoretical language: it was not a *credible threat* for her to punish me.

The idea of the credible threat can be nicely illustrated by a game known as the 'market entry' game. In this game, imagine there's a remote island in the middle of the Pacific, Dough Island, on which there is currently one baker that produces all of the island's bread, cakes, and pastries. It's so remote that it's simply not viable for islanders to import fresh baked goods from the mainland, so the baker has a complete monopoly over the island's baked goods market. As he has a monopoly, he is able to get away with charging higher prices than if he was in competition with other bakers. As a result, the bakery is hugely profitable, and the baker has established for himself a rather lavish lifestyle of weekly pool parties with dozens of beautiful women, and a collection of pimped-out fast cars. An entrepreneurial baker on a nearby island, Yeast Island, however, sees a clear business opportunity: he's going to set up another bakery on Dough Island, and undercut the first baker on price to steal his customers. Naturally, the Dough Island baker is pretty incensed at this prospect – if the Yeast Island baker comes over and sets up a rival bakery, he will be forced to lower his prices, and his profits (and lifestyle) will inevitably suffer. He calls up the Yeast Island baker and makes the following threat: 'I'm telling you this from one baker to another – if you come over here and set up your bakery, I'm going to put my prices so low that you'll be out of business before your first batch of buns has even turned golden brown.' Should the Yeast Island baker take this threat seriously? Is the threat *credible*?

Whether the threat is credible or not depends on whether the Dough Island baker can show that it's in his interests to carry out the threat. If he does carry out the threat once the Yeast Island baker has set up his new bakery, and lowers his prices further than his new rival's, even to the point where he is making a loss on what he is selling, obviously his profits will also suffer. This is clearly not in his interests (at least for now). However, if the Yeast Island baker knows that the Dough Island baker has very deep pockets, and can afford to make a loss on his baked goods for as long as is necessary for him to go out of business (i.e. he adopts what is known as a *predatory pricing* strategy), then the threat is credible, as although he'll make short-term losses, eventually his monopoly of the island's baked goods will be restored. If, following a three-week binge of extravagant parties, the Dough Island baker's financial position isn't so strong, however, and lowering his prices below cost would actually put him out of business, then clearly his threat isn't credible, as going out of business could never be in his interests.

I'll admit that this world of inter-island baking warfare may appear a little far-removed from that of boyfriend – girlfriend relations. Nonetheless, the concept of the credible threat was still relevant to my and Sarah's relationship and can help explain the gradual unravelling of Sarah's 'crazy,' and my parallel transformation into the model boyfriend.

This can best be analysed using a game-theoretical decision tree, showing the possible outcomes that might flow from my decision to either leave the loo seat up, or to put it down:

FIGURE 9: Loo Seat Game (before I fell in love with Sarah)

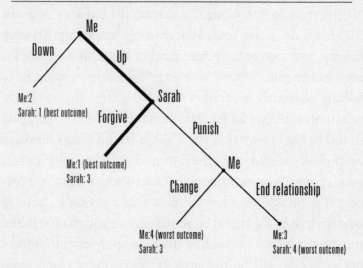

If I put it down, the game ends, and as Sarah hasn't even had to nag me, Sarah gets her best possible outcome (1), and I get my second best outcome (2), as I've had to take the trouble to put the seat down but have avoided her fury. If I decide to leave the seat up, however, the game then progresses to its second phase, where Sarah has the choice of either forgiving me, or punishing me with a nag or minor tantrum. If she forgives me the game ends and I get my best possible outcome (1), as I haven't had to bother putting the seat down, and I've got away with it, and Sarah gets her third best outcome (3), as she's had to suffer putting the seat down herself, but has avoided a potentially relationship-damaging argument. If she decides to punish me the game progresses to its third and final stage, where I have the choice of either complying with her punishment by putting the seat down from that point onwards, or ending the relationship.

What I decide to do at this stage in the game depends entirely on how much I want to be with Sarah. Do I embrace the punishment as a cost of staying with her, or do I value my freedom too much to put up with someone telling me what to do?

In the early days of our relationship I would probably have gone with the latter. As I've explained, when you're with someone new you don't want to be subjected to a life-style overhaul from day one. This means that in the final stage of the game, but at the beginning of the relationship, I would prefer ending the relationship (3) to complying with the punishment (4). As this is the worst possible outcome for Sarah, it is not in her interests to kick up a fuss if I leave the loo seat up, because she knows I am going to break up with her if she punishes me. In other words, her threat of punishment in the event of me leaving the seat up is not credible, as carrying it out will leave her in a worse position (4) than if she forgives me (3). As a result, the likely outcome is that I leave the loo seat up, as I know there is no risk of being punished for my bad habits, and Sarah forgives me (bless her).

Things change, however, when I grow to like Sarah so much that I become more accepting of her punishments. Here, if I leave the loo seat up, and she punishes me for it, I'd much rather change my ways (3) than end it with her (4). This has knock-on effects for whether Sarah decides to punish or forgive me. As she now knows that I will prefer to comply with her punishment than break up with her, she can punish me without fear of the consequences. For me, her threat of punishment is now credible, as I know it is in her interests to actually carry out the threat and punish me for what I have done. This leaves me no choice but to leave the seat down in the first place, making Sarah a happy girlfriend and leaving me in her good books, albeit at a small cost. The decision tree below shows how a shift in preferences in the final stage of the game affects

FIGURE 10: Loo Seat Game (after I fell in love with Sarah)

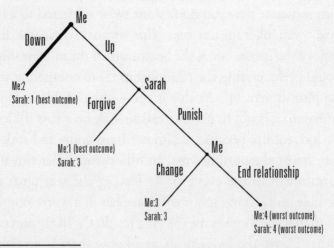

---

30 Also see Chapter 14 on the reasoning behind this process, known as *backwards induction*.

So Freddie's term 'hiding the crazy' seems to be a little unfair. By putting up with our shortcomings in the first few months, girls are just being strategic. No one wants to go out with a lout, but it's also unrealistic for a girl to expect her boyfriend not to put up a little resistance to her naggings before he's even sure there's a serious future with her. Anyhow, it wasn't as if I was doing badly as a result of Sarah's so-called craziness. I rather liked being nagged into good behaviour, not because the nagging was in itself pleasurable, but because of how happy it made Sarah to see me doing things the way she liked. The day I made her bed to her exact specifications she nearly cried.

My investment looked like it was paying off in a big way. I had barely even looked back on my single days, nor did I feel a twinge of jealousy when I saw my flatmates going out on the pull and getting lucky. I was getting strong, stable returns, and they didn't show signs of diminishing.

Chapter 13

That Empty Feeling:
Sunk Costs and Opportunity Costs

I had been going out with Sarah for a year. We celebrated our anniversary with dinner at her flat. I cooked our favourite: bangers and mustard mash. It was my first ever anniversary evening, so I did everything I could to make it special. Partly to give myself a pat on the back for managing to hold on to a girl for a whole year, I had gone for Tesco *Finest* sausages, not the usual 'butcher's choice' ones, made a romantic play list, and even taken out some light bulbs to make her kitchen a little more atmospheric.

It was a nice evening. We chatted about work, about life. We got on well, ate lots of nice food, and then went to bed, too lazy to head out.

I woke up the next morning, pulled on my clothes from the night before and hopped on the bus home. God that journey was beginning to annoy me. The idea that I couldn't just wake up, have a shower, and grab my stuff was growing more frustrating by the day. Other parts of our 'routine' were also beginning to grate. The 'how-was-your-day' text, which I had become accustomed to sending between 6 and 6.30 p.m. every day; spending every weekend together; and actually having to come back from a night out when I said I would, all gnawed at me. I was doing it all out of habit; they were empty gestures.

But I still felt that I had so much to lose. I never had a lonely night, there was always someone to talk to if there was something bothering me, and, of course, I didn't have to worry about getting laid (the occasional tin of cupcakes arriving on a Sunday afternoon was also a good reason to stick around). More fundamentally than weekly treats and an absence of sexual frustration, we just knew each other so well. We could virtually communicate by facial expression alone. We were synchronised; our bodies and minds, our whole lives, were completely entwined with each other. A friend of mine one day noticed, when he was watching Sarah and me cooking together, how little we actually spoke about the cooking as we went along. We knew exactly what the other needed, or when the other thought we weren't doing something quite right, all while having a conversation about our plans for the following weekend. Surely that's not the kind of thing I was going to give up just because having to get the bus back to my flat in the morning meant I had 20 minutes less to spend pottering around in my room before lectures, or because the 20 seconds it took to compose a text message each day while having a cup of tea in front of telly was a bit too much of a hassle? There had to be some good times left in this relationship somewhere. We had put so much into it; it would a shame to waste it all when the best might still be to come.

That said, I was missing out on a lot too. It became all too clear on Freddie's 21st birthday. He and I and about five of his other friends were out celebrating, and based on the rate of beer consumption in the pub beforehand, the night promised to be a big one. Sarah had joined us just before we headed to the regular Wednesday nightclub. We made a beeline for the bar and ordered a round of shots and beer chasers, saw them off, and gave each other testosterone-fuelled high-fives to congratulate ourselves on our latest achievement. As I was making my way around the circle, my hand growing increasingly numb with pain, I noticed Sarah out of the corner of my eye. She wasn't appreciating this at all. She shook her head, looking at me as if I was a dog who had just shat on the carpet. I clicked into 'be-nice-to-Sarah' mode, missed out the last couple of high-fives, and went over to her, my tail between my legs.

'If I knew tonight was going to be like this I would have stayed at home, Will.'

'I am sorry, Sarah, what did you expect? Civilised conversation?'

She didn't say anything, so to break the silence I offered to buy her a drink.

'A cranberry and orange juice thanks.'

'You're not drinking?'

'Last time I checked, cranberry and orange was a drink.'

There was Sarah pulling out one of her classic tactics to make me feel bad about getting drunk – make me feel even more pissed by having a soft drink.

I got the juice for her, we sat down, and had an attempt

at a conversation. I did what I felt was enough to keep her happy, then tried to find an excuse to re-join the boys; it was Freddie I was supposed to be here for, after all.

My state of inebriation had made my excuse-making less persuasive than usual, but she got the picture. 'You can go and join your friends now if you like,' Sarah said, 'go and have fun. Enjoy.'

I leapt up and kissed her goodnight. 'See you tomorrow.'

'But you know you're supposed to be staying at mine tonight? It's Wednesday.'

'Sarah, it's Freddie's birthday, we're going to be out pretty late.'

'Fine, go ahead, just do whatever makes *you* happy.'

'I will.'

That was the most self-assertive thing I had said to her in months.

After Sarah made her (rather melodramatic) exit, I went to re-join the boys. They'd be on their fourth round of shots by now so I'd have a lot of catching up to do, and it was more than likely that there would be some kind of horrific dirty pint waiting for me as punishment for abandoning them for my girlfriend. But they weren't where I had left them. I suspected that they must have already moved on to the dance floor to prey on some poor unsuspecting girls. I scanned the floor for a heaving mass of drunken boys, but to no avail. They were nowhere to be seen.

I wandered around the club hoping to hear a 'Will! Where the hell have you been?' from some dark, thick-aired corner, but it was useless. None of them answered their phones. My night was over by default.

I was woken at about 7:30 the next morning by a clattering in the bathroom. I walked out into the landing to see what was happening, and saw Freddie, sprawled on the floor, clenching a half-eaten Philadelphia and ham sandwich in his fist, gently chuckling away to himself.

'What's so funny?' I asked.

'I don't know,' Freddie drawled, 'this sandwich is just *soooo yummmmmy*.'

It had clearly been a corker of a night. I got him up off the floor and into bed. Somehow I knew even then that I wouldn't hear the end of this, that this one would be spoken about for months, if not years. And, however unfair this may sound, I couldn't help feeling Sarah was to blame.

I sat in the corner of the pub that afternoon, listening to each one of the night's participants taking it in turns to tell the rest how they ended up in their respective precarious situations. One had spent the night on a mattress left out on the street, another had been chased by waiters with chains out of an Italian restaurant (well known for its rumoured links with the Mafia) after he was dared to take a loaf of bread from the kitchen counter. Freddie got lucky with a barmaid. They could barely breathe they were laughing so much. Tears were streaming down their faces. I said nothing. I had nothing *to* say. I just listened as each fresh burst of laughter drowned out the last.

I missed those nights, the ones where you are not quite sure how they are going to end. These boys had managed to blag their way into VIP after I left them, where they let the night run its own unpredictable, riotous course. They didn't have girlfriends texting them every ten minutes to see when they would be getting back home, and they didn't feel bad about having a good time or making a fool of themselves. Being in a relationship seemed to be coming at too high a cost, not necessarily because it was itself making me unhappy, but rather because it was closing off so many different avenues that I was yet to explore.

On a night that Sarah was away, I went out with the boys to see what was down those avenues. Don't get me wrong, I wasn't going out to cheat on her, but having been off the market for a year, it had been quite a while since I had last tried chatting up a girl. I wanted to know whether I still had anything resembling pulling power; I wanted to know what my market value was. We went out to a couple of bars a little further afield than usual to avoid the prying eyes of any gossipmongers.

I felt pretty awkward to begin with, and guilty. Was it wrong that I was talking to these girls as if I wanted to go home with them?

'Don't worry about it,' said Freddie. 'Think of it as going for a test drive with no commitment to buy. Forget about your Volvo estate at home and enjoy the ride, just remember to return the keys at the end.'

Freddie was on home ground. Although he'd always been a faithful boyfriend, he was nonetheless highly skilled at flirting with girls, but always made sure he pulled the plug before he did anything that could technically be classified as cheating. He showed me the ropes, and I, tentatively, went along with it.

I went home alone that night, as planned. But I left the club with something on my mind, something that

I hadn't considered in over a year; an idea of what else might be on offer if I was single again. I realised, after a few false starts, that it wasn't only my girlfriend who thought I was a good deal. My market wasn't limited to just one person – other girls would try and pull me off the shelf, given the chance. The question was, did I value being with Sarah enough to justify having to turn down these other girls?

Being with Sarah cost me time, money, and emotional investment. It also cost me the things that I couldn't have because I was with her, such as spontaneous nights out with the boys and getting with other girls. It was these things that I had to miss out on when I chose how to spend my limited amounts of money and time. Those missed things are what are known, in economic terms, as my *opportunity costs*. Opportunity cost is different to cost in the traditional sense. When we talk about how much something costs we are usually referring to how much money or time we have spent in order to get that thing. Opportunity cost, on the other hand, refers to the things that we can no longer afford to buy or do when we get or do that thing.

A simple example of calculating opportunity cost is when considering whether to make your own packed lunch. A lot of people at university used to bring in their own lunches to save cash. Fair enough: in strict financial terms making your own lunch does save you money. Making your own sandwich and buying your own drink from a supermarket will cost you about £2, whereas the same thing in a café will cost you about £5. But the opportunity cost of making your own lunch is more than just financial; you are giving up the time it takes to make the lunch and being able to eat with friends in a nice café. The question is, from an economic rather than financial perspective, are you willing to give up the time it takes you to make the sandwich and the nice café for the £3 that the D.I.Y lunch is saving you? For me it was definitely no. I'd rather save the money somewhere else. Of course that isn't the same for everyone. It depends entirely on how much you value that nice café atmosphere, and your time, relative to other things. This idea of opportunity cost makes one thing clear: we don't make decisions on how to spend time or money in complete isolation; we need to look at our spending decisions relative to what else is available to make sure we're getting the best deal for ourselves.

Now I just needed to apply this thinking to my predicament with Sarah. If I were to take Sarah in complete isolation, I would say I was happy. As I said earlier, we were a great team. We knew each other better than we knew anyone else in the world. We had put a lot into the relationship, and, although the returns on my investment were diminishing, we might still be able to get a lot more out of it; my returns had not yet been exhausted. But when looking at what I was missing out on, as had become so painfully clear in the pub the day after Freddie's birthday, I wasn't so sure.

I brought this up with Sarah.

'I kind of feel that I've been growing apart from my friends recently. We're only at university once – do you really want to look back on these days at uni and regret all those things that you *didn't* do?'

'So you're saying that you're going to regret being with me?'

'No! Don't be silly, Sarah, I've had a great time with you.'

I realised that this was beginning to sound like a break up, so quickly added, 'I think we've had a great time, *so far*.'

'Yes we have. We've put so much into this, and I know we've had a bit of a rocky time recently but it's going to get better.'

The words 'we've put so much into this' struck a chord. Sarah, I realised, was making the same mistake I had made one night when I was queuing for a club, a club that was so popular that I queued for four hours to get in. Yes, that's right, four hours. FOUR hours. What on earth was I thinking? Who in their right mind wastes most of their night standing out in the cold so they can get into a club stone-cold sober, dance for an hour, and then walk home in the freezing cold? Each time I thought about leaving the queue to find another club, or just go home, I thought to myself, well, I've already waited half an hour, so it would be a waste of my time if I left now. That 'already waited half an hour' then turned into 'already waited an hour … two … three … *four*' hours. The longer I waited, the more willing I became to wait longer simply because the idea of going home empty-handed, having queued for so long, became increasingly unbearable.

If I was thinking more like an economist, and less like the clubber I occasionally try to be, I would have known that I ought to disregard the time I had already spent queuing when deciding whether to wait any longer. That time had been and gone, it was water under the bridge, it was a *sunk cost*. What I should have asked myself was, what do I want to be doing right now? Do I queue for another two hours to get into this club, or do I leave and find somewhere else less busy, or just cut my losses and go home? The time that I had already spent queuing shouldn't even have been factored into my reasoning, however painful it would have been to know that that time had been wasted. You're not going to get that time back, whatever happens. Even if I had pre-paid £10 to go to the club, it still would have made more sense to leave the queue and pay another £20 to get into another club, simply because I would rather pay £20 to get into a club for three hours and still be moderately drunk than £10 to get into a club for an hour of completely sober dancing surrounded by wasted clubbers.

What this meant in terms of deciding my and Sarah's fate was that the attachment to the time that Sarah and I had already spent together, and the bond that had formed between us as a result, shouldn't cloud the fact that what I was missing could make me happier than what I was getting with her. True, it would take time to find someone else, and even more time to get anything like as close to them as I was to Sarah, but that cost, the equivalent of that extra £10 to get into the different club, would be worth it if it filled the void that had been growing inside me.

To put this another way, I needed to stop asking the question 'given that I am in a relationship with Sarah, what reason do I have to break up with her?' and ask instead 'given that I am in a relationship and could be in another relationship, or none at all, what reason do I have to *stay* with her?' Two nice, accommodating people could stay together indefinitely if they continued to ask the former question rather than the latter. They would trundle along together, perfectly happily, for their whole lives. They would get over their differences amicably and be considerate to one another. And yet they could still be missing something and be completely oblivious to it. They might just not have that spark, that bond with someone that makes you feel as though your minds are fused when you speak, and the other's body feel like a natural extension of yours when you touch. But because neither of them had done anything *wrong,* they might think 'if it ain't broke, don't fix it,' and stay together, more through not wanting to lose what they have than thinking they couldn't do any better.

I wasn't going to be one of those people. I was only 21. The time for me to say 'you'll do' and accept the next decent offer to come my way was still a long way off. That meant I needed to forget what had happened between us – disregard my sunk costs, and start looking around me at the other lives I could be leading – consider my opportunity costs. At the moment I was fooling myself that I was doing the right thing by staying with Sarah. I was too attached to the time we had had together, and my fidelity to those sunk costs meant I was turning a blind eye to what else was out there. That was my irrational mind taking hold.

The crucial question for my rational self to answer was: what would someone do if they were to fill my shoes right now and take over my relationship? They would make a decision based on the information and options available at the time, and move on. They wouldn't have the same emotional attachment to the better times that I had enjoyed with Sarah, nor the deluded belief that those times could return to make things better. The right, rational answer was the same as for my dilemma in the queue: had someone joined me after two hours, and weighed up the options, they wouldn't have hung around for long. I wasn't going to make that same mistake again.

It was time for the economist to resume control. It was time to liquidate my investment and buy back into the market. I was ready to be single again.

Chapter 14

Calling It a Day:
Backwards Induction

The next few weeks were horrible. It was as if I had an awful secret that I knew I should tell Sarah, but I couldn't find the right moment (or balls) to do it. Although she didn't know what I was thinking, she could sense it. It's almost impossible to fake warmth towards someone else. Just as Lizzie, the girl who had spurred me on to change my life philosophy, had so cruelly done to me, I was avoiding prolonged eye contact, I quickly retracted any kisses and I generally behaved as if my mind was elsewhere.

I did try to maintain some kind of interest, so as not to give the game away and be cornered into breaking up with her at a time when I hadn't really worked out what I was going to say. But lying has never been a strength of mine, even less so when it involves lying about how I feel towards another person.

For weeks I had been irritated by just about every little detail of Sarah's life: the way she religiously put her bed throw and useless square pillows back on to her bed every morning with total precision, and the way she used to mix her cereal with Shreddies. These were things that I used to find quite endearing once, the peculiar mannerisms I took so much joy in identifying when I first fell in love with her. Now they had become a source of contempt. She didn't deserve this. I needed to think seriously about when I was going to break up with her.

My first thoughts were to give it a few months and let the relationship die a natural death. I could just switch off the life-support machine, and take a back seat as I watched our differences drive us apart to the point where it was almost intolerable to be in the same room together, let alone in a relationship. But what a painful few months that would be, not only in terms of the emotional harm it would inflict on Sarah, but also in opportunity costs – those few months could be spent beginning a new life rather than slowly bringing an old one to its end.

Once again, I went rummaging around in my text books for a solution. One thing that I had learnt from game theory was that if you know how something is going to end, it is often possible to work out the best thing to do now. The process is called *backwards induction*. Unlike the wine bluffer's dilemma in Chapter 6, which was a *one-shot* game, in that the restaurant and I interacted only once, most games are played over many periods, in games known as *repeated games*. In such games, players interact on multiple consecutive occasions and receive their pay-off at the end of each period before playing their next move in the following period. In a repeated game, players form a relationship. They develop reputations for certain kinds of play, and strategies to maximize their individual pay-offs over time.

When using backwards induction, we start where the game ends, the terminal period (t), and work out how people are most likely to behave at that point by looking at what move gives them the biggest pay-off. Then, knowing how people behave in the terminal period, we can work out how they are going to behave in the penultimate period (t minus 1) in anticipation of t. We then look back one further period (t minus 2), and we continue this process until we end up in the current period.

One example of this kind of thinking is the paradox of the 'surprise test.' A teacher says to her students first thing on a Monday morning, 'Now listen very carefully, children, at some point this week we are going to have a surprise test. I'm not going to tell you when it is, because then it wouldn't be a surprise.'

Some of the students then get together at break time to discuss the test.

'How could she do that to us? She could literally set the test at any time. We're going to be on tenterhooks for the rest of the week!'

But one of the nerdier students, Alec, offers some encouragement.

'Don't worry too much, at least we know one thing for sure: it won't be in the last class on Friday, because if she hasn't already set the test by then, we'll know it will have to be in the last class, so it won't be a surprise.'

'Good point, Alec,' says Joscelyn. 'Then, I suppose, if we know that it's not going to be in the last class on Friday, we know that it won't be in the second last class on Friday, either, because if she hasn't given us the test by then, we'll know that it's coming in that class so it won't be a surprise.'

The boy paused, the significance of the chain of reasoning that he had just embarked upon slowly dawning on him. They worked back through the puzzle class by class, day by day, all the way to Monday afternoon, and then to Monday morning, and then the class they had coming up in ten minutes.

'Hold on, does this mean that the surprise test is right now?

'No, it can't be, as then it wouldn't be a surprise test.'

'OK, does that mean there is *no* surprise test?'

They stood there gazing thoughtfully as they tried to come to terms with their newfound superhuman ability to make a test disappear by reasoning alone.

Unfortunately for the students, there was a test. They hadn't made it disappear. It's just that the test wasn't a surprise.

What are we supposed to learn from this story? That the only way of setting a surprise test would be not to warn the students at all? Well, not exactly. The moral of the story, if you can call it a moral (or a story), is that if we are able to reason backwards from a certain point in the future, apparently complex problems can become very simple to solve. I had one such problem, so it was time to put this method to the test.

I started by asking myself whether I knew, for certain, that I would have broken up with Sarah by the time I finished university. The answer was, without a doubt, yes. One of us would probably need a personality transplant for that answer to be any different. Knowing this, I then fast-forwarded to my final day of university, and imagined the scenario where I hadn't actually got around to dumping Sarah yet, but was still certain that I would break up with her before I left the campus for the final time.

I pictured the scene:

It was graduation day. Our parents, having met for the first time over lunch an hour before, proudly looked on while we stood there in our gowns, clutching our second-class degrees. Everyone was thrilled that it was all over, and some remarked on what a great couple we were and how they were already betting on us being the first to get married. I tried to force a smile, but all I could think of was the thing I'd been putting off for the last two years – I had to break up with Sarah within the next three hours.

Our cars were loaded and ready to go. Our parents said their goodbyes, and what a pleasure it was finally to have met, etc. etc. Sarah came over to give me a goodbye kiss.

My conscience spoke to me, 'It's now or never, Will, you said you'd be single by the time you left uni, so just do it, do it now!'

'See you soon, Will. Give me a call when you get home. Safe drive!'

'Ah, Sarah, there's something I've been meaning to tell you, for quite some time, about two years in fact.'

She looked mystified.

I went for it.

'I think we need to see other people.' (Two years of planning and that was all I could come up with.)

'Don't be silly, Will. Is that supposed to be funny or something?'

'No, I mean it. It's just the way you mix your cereal with Shreddies all the bloody time – it's really annoying. And that bloody bed throw of yours – it does my head in!'

She broke down. It was over, just in the nick of time.

Knowing how my graduation-day-from-hell would play out, I then asked myself what I would have been doing the day before these rather perverse series of events unfolded. Would I, knowing that I was going to break up with Sarah for certain the next day, take her out for one final dinner, and relish the final moments I was to have with my soon-to-be-ex?

I imagined us sitting there, for the last time, in our favourite Pizza Express, the scene of our third date.

'Sarah, we've had such a lovely few years together. It's been great knowing ... I mean going to university with you.'

'Will, why are you saying this like we're never going to see each other again after tomorrow? We're going on holiday in a week's time, remember?'

'Ah, yes, of course, the holiday ...'

That option hardly seemed appealing either.

You can see where this was going. Like the schoolchildren trying to predict the timing of their surprise test, the time when I was finally to end it with Sarah was drawing closer, day by day, hour by hour, to the point where I realised I had to do it right there and then.

I'll admit this method of analysis isn't without its flaws. What if I were to change my mind about Sarah before the end of university? How could I possibly say with any conviction that we wouldn't be together by the time we left? In other words, what if my *preferences* changed over time?

Preferences do, undoubtedly, change over time, for better or for worse. Taking them as fixed, as is required if we are to use backwards induction, is therefore pretty unrealistic. If we used backwards induction to make all our decisions on whether or not to stay in a relationship, they wouldn't last beyond their first rocky patch. We would be constantly checking ourselves against the ultimate question: do I want to spend the rest of my life with this person? If the answer was no, as it is perhaps more often than not (unless they are near perfect or when we're near the dreaded You'll Do Horizon; see Chapter 3), that would trigger the chain of reasoning that would inevitably lead to the relationship's untimely demise.

The fact that backwards induction takes our potential pay-offs as certain at any one given time also makes it unlikely to work in practice. Knowing what our best option is going to be at some point in the future is almost impossible to predict with any accuracy. Sarah could well have been the best I'd ever do, so staying with her for ever might have been in my interests. I didn't know, for instance, if I would be able to go and have a wild night out on graduation day minus one and have a better time than if I was still with her. The single route could be even worse: a nightmare of rejection and failure.

It appeared that sound, theoretically elegant economic reasoning had to come at a price. But I knew the fix I was in. I was so certain that a better life lay elsewhere that I didn't really have any time to lose. Prolonging the relationship would only make the eventual break-up harder (if hopefully not as hard as I imagined it would be on graduation day). Staying with Sarah would mean weeks and months in that no-man's-land of being stuck in a relationship that I didn't want, unable to free myself again, or *be* myself again. It had to happen, and it had to happen now.

And so, having made myself as calm and resolute as I could, I went over to Sarah's for the last time. As soon as she opened the door, I knew all the warmth there had ever been between us was gone. There was an air of 'let's get down to business' about the place. She knew what was coming. I didn't, however, expect what came next.

'Oh, Will, I didn't expect to see you here.'

'Hi, Sarah. Just thought I'd come and see how you are.'

'Right, OK.'

She didn't show any signs of inviting me in, so I tried to work up to my delivery of the bad news as carefully as I could.

'Are you going to let me in? There's a couple of things I'd like to talk to you about.'

'Cut the crap, Will.'

'I'm sorry, what?'

'Don't pretend that you haven't come here to break up with me, Will. I could see this one coming weeks ago. Something's changed about you. You've been in your own little world. I just don't think you care about me, or anyone, anymore. So why don't you just grow a pair and do it?'

I was speechless. Being prompted to do what I had been planning for weeks made me doubt whether it was a good idea at all. I looked at Sarah in a way that I hadn't in months; I saw a person with feelings, feelings that I had hurt. She pressed on.

'Well, are you going to say anything?'

Having come over as the one who was going to do the slaying, I now wanted nothing more than to be slain. I just stood there, not knowing what to say or where to look.

'Nothing. How pathetic. Well, you'll be glad to hear that I don't want this to go on any longer either. I think we've both suffered long enough.'

'You're sure?'

'Sure? Will, I know that this is what you want, so there's not much point in wanting anything else. This relationship is over.'

'OK, fine. Good. I'm glad we both see that this isn't working.'

Then I just stood there, as if I was waiting to be offered a cup of tea, or invited through to the sitting room to watch some TV, as usual. But Sarah's body now formed a barrier between me and the rest of her life. Her world was now distinct from mine.

'Bye, Sarah.'

I walked away, assuming, hoping, that the sound of a slammed door would mark my exit. But Sarah closed the door so softly that even the latch springing back into place didn't break the silence.

I expected to leave that flat in a wake of tears and pleas for forgiveness, and a sense of having done something regrettable, but necessary. Yes, what I had done was regrettable, but now seemed far from necessary, and the tears were not Sarah's, but mine.

Chapter 15

Afterword:

Finding Keynesian Love

As you can see, applying economics to the world of dating and relationships didn't really work out for William. By using economics, the thing he thought he understood, he became consumed by his own sense of self-advancement and preservation, forgetting that there was another person, a person with feelings, on the other side of the equation. The thing he was trying to understand, love, remained as much of a mystery to him as when he first embarked upon the Romantic Economist project.

This book was not always destined to end in this way. When I first started writing it, as you saw in the About this Book chapter, I really thought I might be on to something. I wanted to share the ideas that I had about economics and love, and how they might interact, through the medium of a story, loosely based on personal experience. In one of my loftier moments, as ridiculous as this may sound, I even thought that it might spark a new wave of serious academic research on the topic. But, as William's story progressed, so did mine. It progressed in a way which left me doubting not only William's entire romantic philosophy, but also my own assumptions about the nature of love and relationships. It's quite easy to see where I started to go wrong.

I began by saying that the concept of the market of relationships wasn't that original, as it stems from Hobbes's idea that the 'worth of a man' is no more than his 'price'. But the world of Hobbes, which depicts life (in the absence of the state) as 'nasty, brutish and short', perhaps isn't the best model to go on when working out how to attract girls and get them to fall in love with you.

I have since learnt that not only is this a morally dubious way to treat girls, but it is also economically inefficient. Being completely self-interested, concerned only for my own emotional satisfaction and self-preservation, as it did William, left me wholly unsatisfied. I became overly concerned that I wouldn't get back from a relationship at least as much as I put in, so I started to put in even less. I ended up thinking, even though I did like, or even love, the girl that I was with, 'I don't want anything serious, I like being single, best to move on before one of us gets hurt', even though I knew that was not what I really wanted. As a Romantic Economist I was permanently on the defensive, and turned a blind eye to just about any opportunity to get out of the emotional recession that came my way.

That was until I began to write William's story, and came to realise that, however convincing I made the economic rationale for what he was thinking sound, he was doomed for heartbreak from the moment of his 'epiphany' in the aftermath of being dumped by Lizzie. I realised that being like the William at the very beginning of the book, someone who just loved girls with no agenda or concerns about his feelings not being reciprocated, the one who was *easy* to get, could actually be the *solution*, not the problem. However great the risks that approach carried, I couldn't help but feel that it was the right path to choose if I were to achieve sustained, emotional growth. In short, I started to think like a Keynesian.

Keynesians don't believe that balancing a budget — getting back as much as you put in — is the immediate solution to economic malaise. Instead, Keynesian governments try to restore the thing that badly performing economies are generally lacking: confidence. They do this by borrowing money and spending it on public projects, which create jobs, which in turn increases consumption, which creates more jobs, etc., etc. This upwards spiral of investment, production and consumption is known as the *Keynesian Multiplier.* If the multiplier works, the government can actually get back more from the taxpayer than they originally spent, as the rest of the economy, thriving on its renewed sense of confidence, increases production and with it the tax it pays. Keynesian governments therefore get the economy out of recession by acting as its guarantor; they say to the economy, 'We will invest, so you can feel confident in doing so also.'

The mysterious thing about recessions is that nobody wants them to happen, and yet they appear to be as much a fact of life as the Earth going around the Sun. But unlike the Earth's orbit, they are almost entirely man-made phenomena, even though we often speak of them as if they are some kind of natural disaster, completely beyond our control. There's a simple game-theoretic model, known as the 'Stag-Hunt' (or *Game of Assurance*), which explains how something that no one wants can happen so often.

In this game, imagine that there are two cavemen, Throgbor and Grothnuk, hunting in the savannah. They can either hunt for stags or they can hunt for rabbits. If they hunt together, they can catch a stag and share it between them. If they hunt individually, however, they'll only be able to catch a rabbit. That means that if either Throgbor or Grothnuk go hunting for a stag alone, they'll be coming back empty-handed, while the other will be slurping away when he gets home on a rabbit stew for one.

The issue here for both Throgbor and Grothnuk is that if they, expecting to go out for a day's stag-hunting with their fellow caveman, go to the lengths of sharpening their spear, getting their hunting gear together, and making a packed lunch, only to find that the other hasn't turned up as arranged, they are doubly screwed: not only have they wasted all the time and effort preparing for the hunt, but they'll also have absolutely nothing to show for it at the end of the day, and they, and their family, will go hungry. Knowing that there is a risk of this happening, even though getting half a stag is clearly a lot better than one puny little rabbit, if Throgbor and Grothnuk don't trust one another to turn up to go hunting for the stag, they may be inclined to pack their rabbit-hunting nets and settle for the measly stew. Figure 11 is a pay-off matrix showing these different outcomes.

As you can see, if Throgbor and Grothnuk both know that the other wants the stag as much as they do, there

FIGURE 11: The Stag Hunt

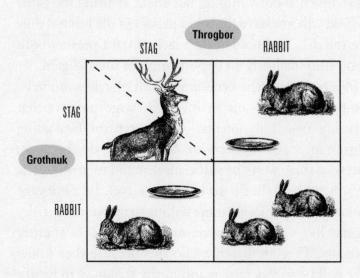

won't be a problem. If Throgbor knows that Grothnuk is going stag-hunting, his best response would be to join him (as he prefer stags to rabbits), and vice versa. The problems arise, however, when the hunters don't have sufficient confidence in the other's intentions. If, for instance, Throgbor only thinks there is a 50 percent chance that Grothnuk is going stag-hunting, he may prefer to go rabbit-hunting, because, if he is risk-averse, he prefers to get a small amount of food for certain to either a lot of food or none at all. Even if Grothnuk definitely wants to go stag-hunting, but is unable to communicate that intention to Throgbor, both hunters might end up getting something that neither of them really wants, even though, had they known the other's intentions, their goals were completely compatible. This game, unlike the one that I was faced with in the *Wine Bluffer's Dilemma,* is therefore not so much about winning, but about assuring the other that you will not leave the other person in the lurch if they take the risk, and not letting a lack of trust prevent both of you from realising an opportunity for mutual gain.

In a recession, the economy is full of rabbit hunters. Companies don't want to invest in large projects that carry big risks but potentially large returns (i.e. going hunting for stags) if others are not going to do the same, otherwise there won't be sufficient demand to justify their investment, and they'll go bust (or starve). In a buoyant economy, companies are more willing to invest in big, risky projects like expanding overseas, or taking over another company. They are happy to do this because they know there will be sufficient demand in the economy to justify that risk and bring them the returns they are looking for. However, when confidence is lacking, companies' instinct for survival takes over, and they simply make do with what will get them by. They invest only in small projects, like reorganising their company rather than taking over others, which are less risky, but also have smaller returns (i.e. rabbit stew). The longer companies remain in this low-risk, small-returns mentality, the less confident an economy becomes, and the more risky it seems to invest in large projects.

Enter the Keynesian government, which is in a unique position to get an economy hunting for stags again. It hunts for stags regardless of whether it thinks others will join. As it has the backing of the taxpayer, the risk of going bust is, although not unthinkable, only a remote possibility. It can therefore invest in large projects, safe in the knowledge that it will not starve, creating the upward spiral in confidence that is required for companies also to go hunting for stags again; it effectively makes a rallying cry to the economy: 'We will be hunting for stags, come and join us.' It cures the economy of the uncertainty that plagues it, and, if all goes well, everyone eats venison steak (with a second or third helping, if they're lucky).

My experiences with girls – during my Romantic Economist experiment – have been very much like this stag-hunt game, only my choices have not been whether to invest in large or small projects, but whether to be *open* or *defensive* with my emotions. Being open is to be honest about your feelings for the other, and embrace them as and when they arise. Being defensive, on the other hand, is to deny the other (and oneself) the expression of those feelings, if they are ever felt. As I have described, I have tended towards the latter, playing 'hard to get' to try to increase my bargaining power, fearing that if I was to give too much away my feelings would not be reciprocated, and I would be made to look overly dependent on the girl (as we all know there's nothing worse than knowing your emotions are flowing down a one-way street). Instead, I have waited for the girls to show the first signs of emotional openness before I have dared to show them myself.

The problem with this approach, as I have discovered, is that it doesn't really work if the girl also follows it and also remains defensive. When neither of us wanted to show any kind of emotional reliance on the other, and seemed determined to live completely independent lives, the result was always unfulfilling, leaving both of us questioning why it was worth being with someone else at all. It was like we were playing a game of chicken. Who would be the first to crack? Who would be the first to say, 'What's going on here? Are we serious? Or are we just playing around?' But neither of us ever did. To do so, or so we thought, would be to lose the prized high ground of emotional invulnerability – and with it any prospect of 'winning' the other person. That conversation only took place once any emotions that we might otherwise have expressed had already faded away, and by which point it was clear that our little 'fling' would have to be brought to rest.

In the stag-hunt game, we were like hunters both yearning to bring home a stag to feast on, but so fearful that the other might not decide to join us that we continued to settle for a dinner-for-one rabbit. In fact, so great was our fear of being open, and going hunting for the stag, that we made the other unsure of whether we wanted to go stag-hunting at all: 'Mmm, this rabbit stew is so tasty!' we would say to the other, trying not to gag, 'It's so much nicer than venison steak!' In other words, remaining defensive made the other person think that we *actually* preferred emotion-neutral flings to emotionally engaged relationships, rather than it just being a temporary phase before opening up that allowed us to assess the likely return on any ensuing investment. This meant that the longer our fling lasted the less we thought our feelings would be reciprocated, even though our desire to reciprocate them ourselves (once the other had shown them), was actually growing. Opposite is another pay-off matrix showing this problem:

FIGURE 12: Finding Keynesian Love

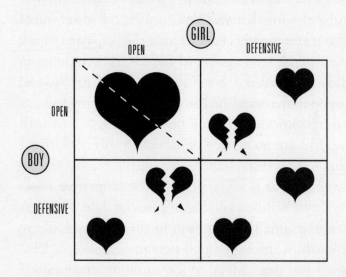

Just like in a recession, each fling or relationship therefore turned into a vicious downward spiral; even though we both increasingly yearned to break out of our emotion-neutral fling, the longer we remained there, the less we thought the other wanted to be open, and the harder it became for us to be open ourselves. Our *apparent* preferences became increasingly disparate from our *actual* preferences, our trust in the other's intentions disintegrated, meaning we became stuck in a situation that made neither of us happy. To make matters worse, this attitude was carried over from one fling to another, meaning that being defensive was fast in danger of becoming a habit.

Clearly, it was now going to require a leap of faith for me to break out of this pattern. I, like a Keynesian government, wanted to restore the trust that I, and the girl I was seeing, had in each others' intentions, to establish the certainty that was so essential to a happy relationship. But the problem with that was that, unlike the government bailing out an economy, I didn't have the taxpayer to back me up. Instead, I was going to have to go stag-hunting regardless of whether I knew the girl would follow, and in doing so make myself vulnerable to having my feelings being unreciprocated and my heart broken. It was with the last girl I am going to write about in this book that I took that self-exposing leap.

I met Rosie, as it so happens, at the same time I was writing about William and Sarah's second date. Needless to say, at the time I'd long been in the habit of looking at relationships through an all-pervasive economic lens. But now I was determined to leave talk of 'undervalued assets' on the market, reducing supply to increase my value, and signalling my 'sweetheart' credentials behind. I wanted to release myself of the burden of balanced emotional budgets, maximising return, and self-preservation. They now all seemed to be more a relic of my youthful, albeit naïve, enthusiasm for my subject, rather than a world view to take into later life. Basically, I decided it was time to try something different.

We'd been dating for a couple of weeks, and we were very much going through the motions; drink, dinner (followed by vertical snog), and then another drink (followed by horizontal snog). I liked her. My gut instinct told me that something good could come of it, but my expectations of something serious happening were pretty low (which, as I mentioned, was more of a carry-over from previous encounters than my actual feelings on how we had gotten on so far).

We reached the familiar third date impasse. I could tell there was something that she was holding back, that she was being defensive. But instead of playing along, and settling in to my defensive mode and waiting for her to budge first, I decided, probably because of that positive gut feeling I had, that I wanted nothing more than to make her happy. I gave myself to her. That didn't mean turning myself into putty to be played with in her hands, it just meant being open. I said, in as many words, 'I like you, I want to spend more time with you.'

I gave, in many ways, more than I could ever, rationally, expect to get back from her. Getting back as much as I put in wasn't really the point. I just wanted, at most, to feel that I had made someone else's life better, to be happy because *she* was happy. I stopped thinking about the intricacies of what signal I should be giving off, the opportunity cost of dating her, and whether I would get a good return on my investment. In short, I stopped thinking only about myself. I took her on nice dates, cooked her dinner, and *listened* to her. The fact that it was taking a bit more time for her to do the same, to open up, didn't bother me. I learnt that she too had had some issues with relationships in the past, and had gone through a string of unsuitable boyfriends, their very unsuitability being her insurance against being hurt by them; you can't get hurt if you don't have any feelings *to be* hurt.

But the more I gave, the longer I sustained my unwavering openness, the more she showed me the person she really was. She, after a time, poured herself into the cracks that I had laid open for her. We fell for each other. I was no longer happy just because I liked the idea of making her happy, but because I was getting to know the real Rosie. The multiplier effect had kicked in; knowing that I was in some way responsible for the flowering and opening up of the person in front of me made me want to give her even more, and she, in turn, gave more back: we became more than the sum of our parts.

All of this wouldn't have been possible, I believe, had I not laid myself out for her to hang her feelings on in the first place. By behaving as if I was blind to the risk of heartbreak, I effectively showed Rosie that I was not even aware of the possibility that I might, myself, break her heart. I built trust between us by showing a child-like innocence, ignoring the potential agony of my feelings not being returned. That then gave her the confidence to do the same. In other words, we built trust and confidence in each other by taking risks with our emotions, risks that we weren't, apparently, aware of.

I feel that it would be appropriate to quote C.S Lewis, from his book *The Four Loves,* at this point:

> To love at all is to be vulnerable. Love anything and your heart will be wrung and possibly broken. If you want to make sure of keeping it intact you must give it to no one, not even an animal. Wrap it carefully round with hobbies and little luxuries; avoid all entanglements. Lock it up safe in the casket or coffin of your selfishness. But in that casket, safe, dark, motionless, airless, it will change. It will not be broken; it will

become unbreakable, impenetrable, irredeemable. To love is to be vulnerable.

Here, Lewis discusses some similar ideas to the ones in this chapter. 'Giving your heart to no one' and 'avoiding all entanglements' is like being defensive with your emotions, the result of which is self-fulfilling; you may avoid heartbreak, but your heart becomes 'impenetrable' and 'irredeemable', or, as I have put it, it becomes harder over time to break out of being defensive the longer you remain so.

J.M. Keynes would have been likely to say something similar on the subject of economic growth. Here's my Keynesian translation of C.S. Lewis' words:

> To grow an economy at all is to take risks. Risk anything and your economy might go into recession and possibly into depression. If you want to make sure your economy doesn't go into depression, you must not take any risks. Wrap it up carefully with spending cuts and small public projects; avoid all long-term investment. Lock it up safe in the casket or coffin of your short-run budgets. But in that casket, safe, dark, motionless, airless, the economy will change. It will not go into depression; it will become stagnant, lack innovation, and become devoid of all investment opportunities. To grow an economy is to take risks.

Keynesian economics and love aren't so dissimilar after all. They work not by balancing budgets, or reducing supply to increase prices, but by inspiring trust, an irrational optimism, or the *animal spirits* in us.

As I've already mentioned, people often speak of recessions like they're a natural disaster, beyond human control, and so we can only expect to mitigate them, rather than prevent them, through careful and considered budgetary adjustments. But actually sometimes the best way to get people to invest and spend their way out of a recession is for the government to spend and invest themselves. It's not an exact science.

Likewise for love. There isn't a secret formula. No, the key to love, as far as I can see, *is* to love.

Acknowledgements

Writing my first book has not been easy, and I couldn't have done it without these people: Charles Elliot, David Isaacs, Elspeth Sinclair, Katrina Porteous, Laura Connell, Sophie Greig, Mark Roberts, Emily Roessler, my parents, and, most of all, Harriet, who has listened to every single word.

William Nicolson is 27 years old and
lives in London. He studied Economics
and Politics at Edinburgh University
and is a solicitor at a City law firm.